Contents

1. Kitchen Tips and Hints
Foods from A to Z; ...... Tips; Home Canning; Sterilizing; Freezing, Cooking and Baking Tips; Cake Decorating; Cake Serving; Cookies; Pies; Breads, Biscuits, Doughnuts; Kitchen Space Makers; Budget Stretchers; Correcting Cooking Calamities

2. Laundry **30**
Stain Removal from A to Z; Washing; Rinsing; Problem Solvers; Washing Machine Tips; Machine Drying; Outdoor Drying; Ironing

3. Looking Your Best **43**
Organizing Closets and Drawers; Shirts; Suits; Gloves; Hats; Hosiery; Handbags; Shoes; Ties and Belts; Underwear; General Clothing Tips; Suede; Eyeglasses; Hair Care; Fingernails; Skin Care; Cosmetic Savers; Personal Care; Jewelry—Its Care and Protection

4. Sewing, Mending and Darning **56**
Buttons; Sewing Savers; Pins and Needles; Threads and Fabrics; Thread Care; Pattern Patter; Knitting Notions; Odds and Ends

5. House Cleaning Furniture **62**
Leather; Vinyl; Slipcovers; Wicker and Wrought Iron; Upholstery; Table Tops; Legs and Seats; Cleaning and Polishing; Stains and Scratches; Cigarette Burns

6. Polishing: Metals and Marbles **67**
Aluminum; Brass; Bronze; Chrome; Copper; Marble; Pewter; Silver; Stainless Steel

7. China and Crystal **71**
Storing; Cleaning; Repairs

8. Clever Cleaning Clues **73**
General Time Savers; Cleaning Pictures; Hard-to-Clean Spots; Bathroom Tips

9. Floors **75**
Tool Care; Floor Protection; Squeaky Floors;
Wood Floors; Linoleum and Tile; Waxing and
Cleaning; Carpets and Rugs; Throw Rugs;
Carpet Stain Removal

10. Walls, Windows and Fireplaces **81**
Wallpaper; Walls; Wood Paneling; Plaster;
Window Washing; Window Protection; Winter
Window Problems; Curtain Care; Shades and
Blinds; Frames and Screens; Fireplaces

11. Paint and Papering Pointers **87**
Mixing Paint; Applying Paint; Painting Tools;
Stairs; Paint Problem Prevention; Time Savers;
Drips and Splatters; Storing Paint; Brushes—
Cleaning and Storing; Painting Furniture; Dec-
orating Tips; Wallpaper; Plaster and Varnish

**12. Energy: How to Conserve It
While Cutting Its Cost** **95**
Lights; Refrigerator; Cooking; Phoning;
Heating; Electrical Appliances; Radiators;
Wood Stoves

13. Recycling Your Discards **100**
Nylons; New Life for Left-Overs; Left-Over Food

14. Household Repairs **103**
Tools; Rust; Screws; Plumbing Tips; Walls;
Plaster; Legs; Making Do; Picture Hanging;
Miscellaneous Ideas

15. Smells and Odors **108**
Kitchen Odors; Food Odors: Brussel Sprouts,
Cabbage, Cauliflower, Onion, Garlic, Fish;
Frying Odors; Garbage Disposals and Cans;
Drains; Refrigerators; Bathrooms; Paint and
Varnish; Closets and Drawers; Creating Pleas-
ant Smells

16. Household Pests **112**
Prevention; Ants; Cockroaches; Flying Insects;
Mice; Mosquitoes; Moths; Silver-fish; Termites

17. Home Office Units **115**
    Mailing Tips; Paper and Stationery; Pens, Pencils and Erasers; Typewriters

18. Plants and Flowers: Real and Artificial — Indoor and Out **118**
    Watering and Nourshing; Cleaning; Grow Your Own; Cuttings; Plant Problems; Vacation Watering; Cut Flowers; Winter Flowers; Artificial Flowers; Outdoor Gardening; Tools; Weeds; Garden Pests; Healthy Soil; Planting and Transplanting

19. Auto Advice **128**
    Conserving Gasoline; Safety; Summer and Winter Car Care; Cleaning; Tar Spots; Tires; Windows and Windshields; Motor Maintenance

20. Child Care **136**
    Bath Time; Baby Clothing; Shoes; Baby Food and Feeding; Kids' Food; Health and Safety; Sickness; Safety; Toys, Games and Playing; Toy Care; Make Your Own; Travelling

21. Pets and Animals **146**
    Birds; Cats; Dogs; Fish

22. Sickroom Tips **149**
    Medication; Temperature Taking; Home Nursing; Patient Comfort; Germ Control

23. Hobbies, Sports and Pastimes **152**
    Art; Fishing; Golf; Hunting; Ice Skating; Photography; Records; Tennis; Stamps; Swimming

24. Odds and Ends **155**
    Re-Use-Its; Emergency Tips; Keep Its; Ease-Its; Save Its

Index **159**

CHAPTER 1

KITCHEN TIPS AND HINTS

There is no way to avoid it. Nothing beats a home-cooked meal. We get a nice, secure feeling whenever we walk into a house and find tempting scents coming from the kitchen. Food is fun! But a lot of people have different feelings about cooking. Some love it, some hate it, and some have no opinion. No matter into what category you fit, here are some hints and tips to make cooking faster, easier and tastier.

Asparagus: Open cans from the bottom so as not to break the tips.

• Fresh asparagus can be cooked in a coffee pot—even an electric pot. Use ½" of salted water and put lid on tightly.

Avocados: To ripen them quickly, place in a bowl and cover with white flour.

Bacon: When broiling bacon on a rack, place a piece or two of bread in the broiler pan. The bread not only soaks up the fat, but also lessens the chances of a "fat" fire.

• Bacon can be cooked by placing the slices on a wire rack over a shallow pan. Bake in a hot oven for ten minutes. This method saves time because you do not have to watch and turn the cooking bacon.

• For a special treat, dip the slices of bacon in beaten egg and coat with cracker crumbs. Fry as you would usually.

Bananas: Green bananas will ripen faster if wrapped in a damp towel and stored in a paper bag.

• To keep bananas ripe, peel them, place upright in a Mason jar, and close the lid tightly. Store in the refrigerator. They will stay ripe for a week to ten days.

• Overripe bananas can be mashed (a blender is ideal) and stored in the freezer for later use in recipes such as banana bread.

Beef (Ground): Ground beef can be stretched by adding bread crumbs either flavored or unflavored or...

• You can add grated raw potato to stretch out a pound of ground beef.

• For quick cooking, poke a hole in each patty before cooking. The hole will seal itself during the cooking process.

• The covers from cottage cheese and sour cream containers can be used as hamburger molds. Wash and dry the plastic tops. Press ground beef into the outside portion. The burgers can be stacked as high as you like and frozen. When you are ready to cook them, take as many as you need. The frozen burgers pop out easily.

Beets: This vegetable can be pan fried just like potatoes. A nice change for your dinner table.

• To peel beets, dip them in boiling water. The skin will split and come off very easily.

Biscuits: When using biscuit mix, use milk, half & half, or cream instead of water. You'll get a fluffier biscuit.

Brown Sugar: The greatest disadvantage to brown sugar is its tendency to harden and get lumpy. To remove those lumps...

• Put the sugar in a double paper bag and place in your oven at a low temperature (250°F). Check every five minutes.

• Place the sugar in a jar and cover with a piece of damp cheese cloth. Screw the jar cover on tightly.

• Place the sugar in a double boiler and steam until soft.

• If you are really in a hurry, grate the hardened sugar.

• To prevent lumps after you open the box, store the sugar in a coffee tin with a plastic lid. Keep it in the refrigerator.

• If you want to store the sugar out of the refrigerator, place a slice of apple in the container or...

• Store the sugar in a jar with dried prunes. The prunes will be super-sweet and the sugar soft, or...

• Place a slice of white bread in the package. Close tightly. The sugar will soften in a few hours. In a hurry?...

• Put the brown sugar in a shallow baking pan. Set a cup of water in the pan with the sugar. Cover with aluminum foil and place in your oven at a low heat (250°F) for fifteen to thirty minutes.

• Out of brown sugar? Make your own. Add one tablespoon of molasses to each cup of white sugar for light, a tablespoon and a half for medium brown, and two tablespoons for dark brown. (White sugar is the result when the molasses has been processed out. In some cases, it is cheaper to make your own brown sugar. Compare the price of a pound of white sugar plus the necessary ounce of molasses against the price of a pound of brown sugar.)

Butter: Here's a money-saving tip to start off. Butter, in any form, whether brick, quarters or tub, sweet or salted, can be stored in your freezer for up to six months. The next time you see a special on butter, don't be afraid to stock up because the butter may turn rancid before you use it. Once frozen, it will keep nicely. But should you find yourself with butter that has turned, don't despair...

• Place the butter in a bowl and let it soften to room temperature. Add two tablespoons of milk. Mix well. Drain off the excess milk

5

which will have absorbed the bad taste. Your butter is fresh again—and fluffy.

• To cream butter and sugar together more quickly, rinse the mixing bowl in boiling water.

• When you need butter that is soft and you don't have any, take the stick and grate it. This method is wonderful for cakes and such. It also creams better when in small pieces.

• To soften butter for spreading, fill a bowl with boiling water. Empty and turn the bowl upside down over the butter dish. In a few minutes, you have butter with spreadability.

• Want to double your butter and save a little money? Take one pound of butter (either sweet or slightly salted) at room temperature. Slowly beat in two cups of evaporated milk. Pour into a pan and chill. Results—two pounds of butter for the price of one!

Buttermilk: An excellent substitute for sour cream on your baked potatoes. And with fewer calories, too.

• Now you can make your own very easily. Buy one quart of buttermilk and a box of powdered milk. Using quart jars that have been washed and sterilized, add a cup of buttermilk to each jar. Mix the powdered mix according to package directions. Now add the prepared powdered milk to each jar. Fill to the top. Add a dash of salt to each jar and cover them. Leave out overnight and then chill in your refrigerator. You'll have four quarts of buttermilk. As you pour out the buttermilk from each jar, just keep adding more prepared powdered milk. You'll never run out, and you'll never have to buy another quart of buttermilk again.

Cabbage (Red and White): To make sure all insects are out, soak cabbage in a bowl of salted water before cooking.

• To keep red cabbage red, add a dash of lemon juice after cooking.

Casseroles: When you freeze casseroles, why tie up a dish? Line your casserole with foil. Place in the freezer. When the casserole is frozen, lift it out and tighten the foil. Back into the freezer. Presto! Another free casserole dish.

Catsup: Can't get a new bottle started? Push an ordinary drinking straw down to the bottom of the bottle. This will allow enough air into the bottle, and the catsup will flow out smoothly. No more slapping the bottom of the bottle.

Cauliflower: A squirt of lemon juice added to the cooking water will keep the vegetable from discoloring.

• Need a quick cheese sauce? Heat a can of condensed cheddar cheese soup with a quarter cup of milk or cream for a richer sauce.

6

Celery: Your celery will stay fresher and crisper longer if you store it in a paper bag rather than the cellophane wrap the stores use. Leave the outer greens on; remove them only when you are ready to use the celery.

• Want to dry the celery leaves for later use? Place them in a paper bag. Fold over the top and poke a few holes in the bag. (A fork is perfect for hole punching.) Keep the bag in a dry place. The celery will dry out perfectly.

• For extra crisp celery, soak the stalks in iced water for a few minutes before serving.

Cheese: Cheese will keep much fresher much longer if you slice it into sections. Store the sections in a tightly-covered jar in your refrigerator. This method eliminates the drying process.

• You can also preserve your cheeses by wrapping them in cheesecloth moistened with white vinegar.

• To cut cheese, use a DULL knife that has been dipped in boiling water. You'll get a finer slice and no crumbling.

• When cheese becomes moldy, place it in a jar with a few lumps of sugar. Cover tightly. The sugar will absorb the cheese mold. By the way, cheese mold is not harmful. It is what made the cheese in the first place. Most people just find it unappealing and bitter-tasting.

• Hate grating cheese everytime you need some? Grate in large quantities and store in a plastic bag in your freezer. When you need some, just take the amount necessary. It will thaw in fifteen minutes or less.

Chicken: Boning chicken is much easier if you do it while the bird is still slightly frozen.

• Frying chicken is best done in an old-fashioned skillet because the heat spreads slowly. For perfectly fried chicken, use hot shortening about one inch deep. Put in the chicken pieces and put the lid on. Turn each piece only once.

Cinnamon Toast: Keep a mixture of cinnamon and sugar in a large shaker. The ideal mixture is one to one, i.e., half a cup of cinnamon to half a cup of sugar.

Coffee: Line the basket of your coffee pot with a facial tissue. It will filter out the bitter taste, and it will make removing the grounds easier.

• If you don't like the taste of reheated coffee, put the left-over amount in a thermos. The coffee will stay piping hot without reheating.

• If you don't like the instant taste of instant coffee, try this method: Boil the water in a pot. Add the powdered coffee and bring the solution to a second boil. Turn off the fire and let the coffee steep for a minute or two. The second boil takes away the "instant" flavor so many people object to.

Cooking Oils: Olive oil will stay fresher longer if you add a cube of sugar to the bottle.

• All cooking oils should be stored in the refrigerator after they are open.

• You can make your own olive oil by taking four large, unstuffed black olives and adding to a cup of ordinary oil. Pour into a jar and cover tightly. Store the oil in the refrigerator for a week.

Corn: To remove the silk from fresh corn, wipe each ear with a moist terry towel. Use a downward motion. All the silk will come off.

• Never throw away an extra ear of corn. Wrap in foil and store in your refrigerator. You can scrape off the corn to use in pancakes, gravy, anything you like.

• Hate the messiness of buttering corn on the cob? Use a crust of bread and smear it with butter. Apply the butter with the bread.

Cottage Cheese: When storing, keep the container upside down in your refrigerator. The cottage cheese will last twice as long.

Cream: To prevent splatters while whipping cream, take a piece of foil and make holes for the beaters. Slip them through and into your electric mixer. Cover the bowl with the foil.

• Adding a few drops of lemon juice while whipping heavy cream will speed up the process.

• Use powdered sugar instead of granulated sugar. This gives you a fluffier, longer-lasting topping.

• You can whip heavy cream ahead of time if you use corn syrup and not sugar as your sweetener.

• To make sure your cream whips, chill the bowl and the beaters in your freezer. Place the bowl of cream in a bed of cracked ice.

Doughnuts: Love doughnuts, but hate the greasy taste? Add a clove to the fat you use to fry them in. No more greasies.

Eggs: Fried eggs won't splatter grease if you sprinkle a little flour into the hot fat. The eggs will brown nicely, too.

• To keep aluminum pots from turning dark when boiling eggs, add a tablespoon of vinegar to the cooking water.

• When your favorite recipe calls for eggs, separate the whites from the yolks. Add the yolks and beat the whites. Then add them. The result—a fluffier cake, waffle, whatever.

• Cracked egg? You can still boil it. Wrap it in foil first.

• When slicing hard boiled eggs, dip your knife in water first. No more broken yolks.

• Egg whites beat up quicker and drier if you add a pinch of salt and let the whites stand until they are at room temperature.

• Short one egg? Substitute one teaspoon of corn starch.

• Your favorite recipe calls for egg yolks only? The egg whites can be stored in your freezer for up to a year. And they can be thawed and frozen again.

• Seven to eight egg whites equals one cup.

• Not sure your eggs are fresh? Fresh eggs are rough and have a chalky appearance. Still have your doubts? Place the eggs in a bowl of cool salted water. If they sink, they are fresh; if they float to the top, they are bad.

• Hard-boiled eggs will spin, raw eggs will not.

• If you pierce the end of an egg with a pin, it will not break when placed in boiling water.

• Eggs stuck to the carton? Wet the box and the eggs will come loose without any cracking or breaking.

• Have trouble separating eggs? Use a small funnel. The white will slip through, the yolk will stay put—and will not break.

• Brown and white eggs are of the same quality.

• When you break open an egg and find a blood spot, it does not mean the egg is bad. If the spot bothers you, remove it.

• Medium-sized eggs are best for baking. Larger eggs cause cakes and such to fall when cooled.

• Shells can be removed easily from hard-boiled eggs if you rinse them in cold water before peeling.

• Leftover egg yolks? You can keep them fresh in your refrigerator for several days if you cover them with water. Leftover egg yolks make attractive garnishes if boiled. They can also be beaten slightly and added to boullion.

• For perfect poaching, use boiling water to which salt and one tablespoon of vinegar or lemon juice have been added. Break the eggs into this and stir ever so gently.

Fish: Fried fish will leave less of an odor if you soak it first in lemon juice for thirty minutes and then fry.

• Thaw frozen fish in milk. This draws out the "fishy" taste and adds that fresh-caught flavor.

• To store fish, clean it and place it in a tray of water and then freeze it.

• Unless you are planning to fry or stuff your frozen fish, don't bother defrosting. Bake as it is. Saves time.

Garlic: If you like to flavor your sauces, soups and gravies with a clove of garlic and can never seem to find it when you want to remove it, spear the garlic clove with a toothpick.

- No garlic press? Lay the clove between two sheets of wax paper and tap lightly with a hammer.
- Garlic will last "ages" if peeled and kept in a small jar of oil. Want to have a steady supply of garlic handy? Place an unpeeled clove in a little water until roots appear. Then plant the clove in a small flower pot.
- When a clove is hard to peel, run it under hot water first.
- Garlic can also be stored in your freezer.

Gelatin: How to unmold without ruining them? Coat the pan with mayonnaise or a small amount of salad oil. Still stuck? Dip the mold in a pan of boiling water. Repeat the process until the gelatin slips out easily.

Gravy: Here's a tip to make your gravy even more flavorful. When you are roasting, place the flour you will use for thickening in a custard cup or foil pie tin and let the flour roast with your meat. It will brown nicely and absorb the flavor of the meat.

- No more lumpy gravy! Put one or more cups of cold water in a jar with a tight lid. Add the flour and shake vigorously.
- If your gravy looks too pale, add a few drops of steak sauce or Worcestershire sauce.
- If your gravy is too thin, add instant potato flakes.
- If your gravy is too greasy, add baking soda in small amounts until you achieve the proper consistency.

Ham: To remove the rind, slit it lengthwise on the underside of the ham before placing it in the oven. As the ham cooks, the rind will pull away and remove quite easily.

- To keep canned hams fresh once they have been opened, keep the upper part of the tin. Take the unused portion of the ham, put it on a plate and place the upper part of the tin over it. Store in the refrigerator.

Lemons: Store fresh lemons in a tightly sealed jar of water in your refrigerator. They will give you much more juice than when first purchased.

- Before squeezing a lemon, grate off the rind and store in your refrigerator. You never know when you need rind in a hurry.
- To get the maximum amount of juice from a lemon, place it in hot water for fifteen minutes or warm it in your oven for a few minutes. Finally, roll the lemon along your counter top.
- For just a few drops of fresh lemon juice, pierce the fruit with a toothpick and squeeze out the amount you need. The lemon will not

10

dry out.

• Just need half a fresh lemon? Save the other half. Put a small amount of water in a saucer. Put the lemon, cut side down, in and store in your refrigerator.

(NOTE: The above tips work equally well for any citrus whether limes, oranges, grapefruits.)

Lettuce: Lettuce stays crisper longer if stored in paper bags in your refrigerator's vegetable bin.

• Another way to keep crispness—cut the head in half. Place both halves in a bowl of water and store in refrigerator. Change the water every five days. By using this method, you keep lettuce for at least seven days, ten days tops.

• No more drippy salads! Line your salad bowl with paper towels. Add the torn lettuce. Cover with more toweling. The paper will absorb all the moisture.

Meringue: Here are some secrets to a good meringue...

• Egg whites should be at room temperature. Use three for each pie and three level tablespoons of sugar for each white. Sounds like a lot of sugar, but it makes a super meringue.

• Make sure the meringue touches the edges of the pie plate. Brown on the middle shelf of your oven. Let the meringue cool away from drafts. Meringue should cool slowly: when the meringue is as brown as you want it, turn off your oven and leave the door open. The pie, still in the oven, will cool slowly, very slowly.

• And for the perfect cut, dip your knife in hot water or give it a thin coating of cooking oil.

Milk: No more messy ring in your saucepan when you heat milk. Rinse the pan with cold water first.

• Never discard sour milk. It is excellent for cooking. Your cakes and pancakes will be fluffier than ever if you use sour milk.

Nuts: A tasty treat and full of protein, too, but, oh, can they be difficult to shell! Not any more. Here are some surefire tips that save time, trouble and broken nut meats:

• To open a fresh coconut, puncture the eyes with an ice pick. Drain out the milk. Place the coconut in a shallow pan and bake at 350°F for forty-five minutes to one hour (until the shell begins to crack). Cool and then tap it sharply with a hammer. The shell will fall apart very nicely. Then you can pick out the meat with a knife.

• To shred coconut, scrape off the brown with a paring knife. Break the meat into smallish pieces and place in your blender with a bit of the coconut milk. Set your blender on "grate".

• To peel almonds once they have been shelled, drop the nuts in boiling water for ten to fifteen minutes. The skins will pop right off.

• To shell Brazil nuts, bake them at 350°F for fifteen minutes. Or you can freeze them. Crack and shell.

• To shell chestnuts, cut a slit in the flat side of each nut. Put them in a saucepan with water to cover them. Boil the nuts for ten minutes. Using a small knife, peel off the shell and membrane.

• To shell walnuts so that the meat comes out whole, soak the nuts in salt water overnight.

Onions: Like the flavor of onions in your salads, but not the onions themselves? Cut an onion in quarters and leave it in the salad for an hour or so. Remove the quarters when you serve the salad.

• Need just half an onion for a recipe? Slice the onion in half before peeling. Wrap one half in plastic wrap and store in your refrigerator. Peel and use the other half.

• Want to avoid tears while preparing onions? Turn on the back burner of your gas stove. The flame burns up the fumes.

• Another way to avoid tears is to breath with your mouth open. You can also stop crying over onions by placing them in your refrigerator for several hours before using them.

• To store onions in a bin, wrap them separately in pieces of aluminium foil. This will keep them from sprouting and turning soft and mushy.

• Onion will brown faster if fried with paprika.

• When peeling an onion, slice off both ends and slice down through the skin. You can remove the skin in one piece.

• One tablespoon of dried minced onion equals the flavor of one medium onion.

Parsley: Fresh parsley will stay fresher longer if you rinse it in cold water, shake dry, and store in a tightly covered container in your refrigerator.

• Parsley rinsed in hot water before chopping has more flavor.

• Chewing a sprig or two of parsley is a great way to freshen your breath.

• Parsley can also be frozen. Take your fresh parsley, rinse it well and let it dry. Put the parsley in a plastic bag and store in your freezer. When the parsley is frozen, chop it. Return it to the bag and back into the freezer. You will always have freshly chopped, bright green parsley available.

Pasta: Any pasta, noodles, macaroni will look more buttery if you add a few drops of yellow food coloring to the cooking water. Saves having to use butter which saves on calories!

• To keep cooked pasta from sticking together, add a drop or two of oil and toss.

Pepper: Have trouble filling your pepper shakers? The next time you use up a box of salt, save it. Empty the pepper into the box. All you have to do is remove the spout and use a funnel. (NOTE: Buy the largest can of pepper you can. It is more economical.)

Potatoes (white, sweet and instant): To prevent overcooked potatoes from becoming soggy when you add milk, use powdered rather than liquid milk.

• You can bake potatoes in a hurry if you boil them in salted water for ten minutes and place in your oven, or...if you cut a thin slice from each end before placing them in the oven, or...if you insert a nail in each. This will shorten the required baking time by fifteen minutes.

• Sliced more potatoes than you need? Cover them with cold water and add a teaspoon of vinegar. They will keep in your refrigerator for up to four days.

• Boiled potatoes will stay snowy white if you add one teaspoon of lemon juice to the cooking water.

• Need to reheat a baked potato? Dip it in water and bake at 350°F for twenty minutes. That fresh-baked flavor remains.

• Sweet potatoes can be stored for long periods in a warm, dry cabinet.

• Adding a little cooking oil to the water when boiling potatoes will prevent a sticky ring on your pot.

• Tired of your baked potatoes rolling around the oven? Bake them in muffin tins. This also makes them easier to remove.

• Potato skins should be rubbed with a little cooking oil before baking.

• For crisp French fries, allow the potatoes to stand in cold water for thirty minutes before cooking.

• Mashed potatoes whipped with cream cheese rather than butter contain fewer calories.

• Leftover mashed potatoes can be shaped into patties, frozen and fried whenever you wish. You can also flavor the potatoes with chopped onion, garlic, anything you like.

• For extra tasty instant mashed potatoes, use the cooking water from your boiled vegetables. This is a great way to get the benefit of the vitamins that boil away in vegetable water.

• Potatoes done before the rest of your meal? Drain the water from the pot and cover with a towel.

• When grating potatoes, insert a fork in one end. Saves scraped knuckles.

• When potatoes are cut well in advance of cooking, keep them in a plastic bag in your refrigerator.

• Add cut potatoes to cooking water only after it has started to boil.

• Potatoes can be baked in half the time if you remove the centers with an apple corer.

Pumpkin Pie Spice: Here's a money saving tip: Each teaspoon of commercially prepared pumpkin pie spice contains one half teaspoon of cinnamon, a quarter teaspoon of ginger and an eighth teaspoon each of nutmeg and cloves. Now you can mix your own instead of buying it.

Raisins: To keep dried raisins fresh for a long period of time, store them in a covered jar in your refrigerator.

• "Stuck together" raisins will separate if steamed briefly over boiling water. You can also use this method to plump raisins for cookies and cakes.

• To keep raisins from sinking to the bottom of your cakes and pies, coat them with flour first.

Rice: If you add a few drops of vinegar to the cooking water when boiling rice, your aluminum pot will not turn dark...and the flavor of the rice will not be changed.

• A slice of dry bread placed over cooked and drained rice will absorb all the moisture, leaving your rice dry and fluffy.

• You can reheat leftover rice by putting it in a sieve and steaming it over boiling water.

Sausage: Sausages will shrink less and not break if you boil them about eight minutes before you fry them. You can also roll them in flour before you fry for the same results.

• To keep frozen sausage from sticking to the paper, run the package under cold water first. No separation problems.

• To absorb the heavy grease produced by frying sausage, add a tablespoon of lemon juice to your frying pan. The citric acid neutralizes the fat.

Shellfish: Clams are easier to open if you pour boiling water over them first. Or you can rinse your shellfish in cold water, put them in a plastic bag, and store in your freezer for at least an hour.

• Like fried shellfish but not the messy clean-up? Do your frying in an empty two or three pound coffee can. Fill the can one-third full with oil and heat. When you are done frying, put the plastic lid on the can and save the oil for your next frying session.

Soup: If your soup is too greasy, add a lettuce leaf. It will absorb the fat.

• To thicken watery soups, add instant mashed potatoes.

Tea: To freshen iced tea which has clouded during refrigeration, add a little boiling water before serving.

• Easy iced tea recipe: Place tea leaves or bags in a jar of cold water and cover. Leave the jar in the sun for several hours. Delicious self-brewing tea!

• For some reason, tea tastes better when brewed in a coffee can. Just pour in the boiling water, add the tea, and cover with the plastic top. Brew to the desired strength.

• For a different flavor, dissolve lemon drops or hard candy instead of sugar in your tea.

• For instant iced tea, add a small amount of boiling water before adding the cold. The crystals will dissolve instantly and give a better flavor.

• For extra strong tea, add a pinch of baking soda.

• One pound of loose tea makes about two hundred cups.

Tomatoes: To peel tomatoes quickly and easily, dip them in boiling water until the skin splits.

• Slightly green tomatoes will ripen nicely if left on a window side where the sun can get to them.

• To scoop out tomatoes without making a mess of it, use a serrated grapefruit spoon.

• To thicken stewed tomatoes, use corn starch instead of flour. And tomatoes stewed in sugared water have a less acidic taste. Use a teaspoon of sugar for each quart of water.

Turkey: Never thaw a turkey at room temperature. Defrost it in the refrigerator. This method takes two or three days but greatly reduces the possibility of food poisoning.

• Toast the bread used for stuffing. You get a crunchier dressing. And don't pack the stuffing in too tightly as the turkey juices cause the dressing to swell during cooking.

• To speed up the necessary cooking time, cover the turkey with aluminum foil.

Waffles: Did you make too many waffles? Don't throw them out. Freeze the leftovers. They can be reheated either in your toaster or under the broiler. Makes for a quick breakfast treat.

Wine: Any recipe that calls for water (i.e., gravy) substitute red cooking wine.

• Wine left over from a fancy dinner? Save it for cooking, Or...leave it on your kitchen counter, corked loosely, until it turns to wine vinegar.

Yogurt: Love yogurt? Thinking of buying one of those fancy yogurt makers? Don't bother. Here's how to make your own yogurt:

• Bring one quart of milk (either whole or skim) to a boil. Let it cool until you can hold your finger in it comfortably. Pour into a large mixing bowl and add two tablespoons of plain yogurt. Cover the bowl and place it in a warm spot for about five hours. A warm spot can be your radiator, your electric buffet server, or even your oven set at 250°F.

Freshness Hints and Tips

• Keep a dry sponge in the vegetable crisper of your refrigerator. It absorbs excess moisture. Wring the sponge out every day or two.

• To crisp up soggy potato chips, cereal and crackers, spread them on a cookie sheet. Place in a 250°F oven for five to ten minutes. In damp, humid weather, don't let them get soggy. Store them in your refrigerator in a tightly covered container.

• No more clogged salt shakers if you put six or seven grains of rice in the shaker.

• When you can't find your corkscrew, run the bottle neck under hot water. The glass will expand and the cork will slide out.

• To keep freshly cut fruit from browning, toss with a few drops of lemon juice or cover in a syrup made of equal parts of sugar and water that has been boiled until thick.

HOME CANNING

The last several years have seen a renewed interest in the ancient art of home canning. The more modern process of home freezing is another hot topic. For those of you who are following this trend toward do-it-yourself food, here's some information Grandma never thought to tell you:

• You can avoid the formation of scum on your canned foods if you add two tablespoon of vinegar to the water you use to sterilize the jars and bottles.

• When pouring hot fruits and vegetables into glass jars and bottles, rest them on a towel that has been rinsed in cold water. This will keep the glass from cracking.

• Need a cherry pitter? A sturdy paperclip is ideal.

• To prevent mold from forming when you can pickles, place a small bag of mustard seed on top before you seal the jar.

Fruit

• Here's an easy recipe for making grape juice: Stem one pint of grapes and place in a hot, sterilized quart jar. Add one cup of sugar. Cover with boiling water. Seal the jar and leave upside down over night. Store in a cool, dark place until you are ready to drink it. Grape juice made this way has both excellent flavor and color.

• When you are canning pears, you do not have to peel them. Scald them as you would tomatoes or peaches. The skins will slip right off.

• To prepare fresh pineapple for canning, forget about peeling, coring, and what have you. Slice off the top of the fruit and cut it into quarters. Then scrape the fruit downward with a tablespoon. Instant crushed pineapple!

Sterilizing

• Melting paraffin to seal jams and jellies is sloppy and what a residue it leaves in the pot! Break the wax into small pieces and drop them into an empty milk carton. Place the container into boiling water until the paraffin melts. Pour off the amount you need. When you are done, you can either throw the container out or keep it in your refrigerator until you are ready to make another batch of jams and jellies. And to keep the paraffin liquid, leave the container in the hot water.

• Sterilizing does not necessarily mean boiling. Wash and rinse your canning jars and bottles thoroughly. Place them on a pan and put them in a cold oven. Set the oven at 250°F and leave for ten minutes. Turn the oven off. Not only are the jars and bottles fully sterilized, but they will also stay that way for quite a while.

• Canning jars and bottles can be a hassle to remove from the boiling water used to sterilize them. Tongs are not always as secure as they should be. Try wearing a heavy leather glove for this task. The leather will give you a better grip while protecting your hand.

• Before sealing jams and jellies, place a piece of string across the mouth of the container. Pour the paraffin over the top. When you are ready to use the homemade goody, you can remove the seal very easily by giving both ends of the string a good tug.

Jams and Jellies

• If your jelly is not setting the way it should, put the jars in a pan of hot water and place in a warm oven, about 250°F for a few minutes.

• Before making jams, rub the inside of the pot with plain cooking oil. This will prevent sticking and burning.

• Jelly making means straining the fruit through cheese cloth. Secure the cloth bag to a suitably sized embroidery hoop. The bag stays open, and you can pour the fruit through without spilling.

• The self-adhering tabs used in offices to mark file folders are good for labeling your canned goods and jellies.

• When you want to clear the jelly you are making from fruit parings, boil the mixture with freshly broken eggshells before you add the sugar. The sediment adheres to the shell.

Freezing

• Love to store fresh peas in the freezer but hate to shell them? You really don't have to. Pop the pods into boiling water and then into cold. This forces the pods open and makes for really fast shelling.

• Unbaked fruit pies can be frozen for up to two months. Baked fruit pies can be frozen for up to six months.

• Whenever you add to your freezer, store under what is already in there. This insures that you will use the earlier additions first. And always mark what you are freezing with the date you put it into storage.

• Empty one and half gallon milk cartons make good freezer containers. You can force open the spout portion to add the food and then seal again with staples.

• When you are freezing ground beef for hamburgers, make the patties first. When you are not, form the meat into a flat shape rather than a round ball. This will make defrosting faster.

• To protect plastic freezer bags from punctures, place them in old nylon stockings. Make a handle by knotting the toe to the top portion.

• To freeze individual portions of soup, place the stock in ice cube trays. One or two cubes is a good single serving.

• There are a couple of ways to make sure all the air is out of your freezer bags. Hold the top of the bag closed—just tight enough so that the air can escape. Place the bag in a pot of water. The water pressure will force the air out. You can also use the exhaust from your vacuum cleaner to draw the air out.

• Here are some tips for paring ears of corn. To hold the ear steady, push a short nail through a jar lid. Secure the ear to the nail. While paring, have the ear in a fairly large baking pan. This will keep the kernels from flying all over the place. For really quick paring, sharpen the edge of a metal shoehorn. The curve is just right for an ear of corn.

• Empty milk containers are ideal for freezing fresh fish. Add the fish and then water to cover. Staple the top shut. There is no freezer burn with this method.

• Most fruits and berries will process much faster if they are frozen first. Cranberries, blueberries, etc. Pate is also easier if you freeze the liver and then put it through your food processor.

COOKING AND BAKING TIPS

Cakes

• Many recipes still call for cake flour which can be hard to find. Not to worry. For each cup of all-purpose flour you use, remove two tablespoons and replace with two tablespoons of corn starch. That gives you cake flour.

• When you use a cake mix and the pans must be floured, use the mix. Put the excess back into the mixing bowl.

• When you are short of cupcake tins, you can improvise. Place the paper holders on can lids and fill with batter. The lids can then be lined up on cookie sheets.

• Do without air holes in your cakes—pour the batter into the baking pan through a slotted spoon.

• To cut down on your baking time, sift flour and sugar into their cannisters. This means no more sifting for individual recipes.

• If you do a lot of baking, especially when you use one particular recipe over and over again, prepare the dry ingredients in advance. The dry batches can be stored in empty one pound coffee cans. When you want to bake, empty the contents into a mixing bowl and add the liquids in their required order.

• Fruits and nuts will not sink to the bottom of the batter if they are heated in the oven at a low temperature (250°F) for a few minutes. And for even distribution in the batter, roll the fruits and nuts in flour before adding to the batter.

• To give a plain white cake a special flavor, streak a teaspoon or two of instant powdered coffee through the batter. You can get a nice marbled effect and a delicious mocha flavor.

• For individual steamed puddings and cakes, use empty beer cans. With a can opener, remove the top lid. Add the batter and seal with aluminum foil. When done, you can remove the contents by taking off the bottom lid and pushing the cake or pudding out gently. For larger portions of steamed goodies, empty coffee cans of whatever size, are excellent.

- An ice cream scoop is perfect for filling muffin and cupcake tins. The scoop is of the right size and there will be no dripping.

- To remove a cake from a tin when it is sticking, hold the pan over a low flame for a few seconds.

- Need a ring pan in a hurry? Place an oven-proof glass in the center of an ordinary cake pan.

- For commercial chiffon cake mixes, substitute orange juice to which the juice of half a lemon has been added for the required liquid. You will get a truly delicious cake.

- To keep cakes fresher longer, cut the cake in half. Take from the inside. Push the two halves together and wrap in foil.

- You can also store your cakes in a tightly covered container with a sliced apple. The apple will keep the cake moist and fresh.

- Your cakes will not stick to the pans if you wrap a towel dipped in hot water around the pans when you take them from the oven.

- Do not bake your layer cakes one pan directly over the other. Stagger the pans. If the cake browns too quickly, place a pan of water on the top rack of your oven. To prevent browned edges on small cakes, place a pan of cold water on the bottom shelf of your oven.

- When your cake batter is too stiff, add a beaten egg, a little at a time.

- To avoid white flour deposits on chocolate cakes, dust the pan with cocoa rather than flour.

- Out of solid chocolate? No problem. Mix four tablespoons of powdered cocoa with ½ teaspoon of melted butter.

- Fruit cake will not dry out if you wrap it in a piece of cheese cloth dipped in sherry or bourbon or rum.

- Cakes sticking to the plate? Dust the plate with powdered sugar before you put the cake on it. And powdered sugar can be used to keep the frosting from sticking to waxed paper wrapping. Sprinkle powdered sugar over the waxed paper before wrapping.

- To "season" new cake tins, coat them with margarine and place in a moderate (300°F) oven for fifteen minutes.

- When cutting frosted cakes, run the knife under boiling water first.

- Cakes too crumbly to ice properly? Pop the cake in your freezer until it is firm and then spread the frosting.

Cake Serving

- When slicing round cakes, you will get neater servings if you first cut a circle in the middle of the cake.

• Heavy-duty nylon thread makes cutting angel food cake very easy. Draw the thread through the cake in a sawing motion.

• If your favorite cake has dried out, you can still use it. Put what is left into the top of a double boiler and pour half a cup of heavy cream over the mixture. Cover and warm over a low flame for fifteen minutes. The results? A rich pudding-like mixture.

• To revive stale cake, dip slices in cold milk and heat in a moderate (300°F) oven for five to ten minutes.

Cake Decorating

• Marshmallows can be cut into different shapes and dipped in food coloring and then used as cake decorations.

• When placing prepared decorations on your cake, use broad tweezers. This keeps your fingers clean and the icing smooth.

• When you use pre-cut patterns to trace designs on your cakes, dip the pattern in water first. It will not stick to the cake when you remove it.

• A toothpick dipped in food coloring makes an easy-to-use pen and ink for writing messages on your cakes.

• Squeeze-type catsup and mustard containers are very handy for decorating cakes.

• Save the juice from maraschino cherries. Soak shredded coconut in the juice. And remember, the longer coconut soaks, the darker the color becomes.

• For a quick frosting, remove the cake from the oven and turn the heat off. Cover the cake with chocolate mint patties and return the cake to the oven until the candy melts.

• Simple, uncooked chocolate frosting will have a fudge-like flavor if you brown the butter before adding it to the other ingredients.

• Have some left-over potatoes you don't know what to do with? Use them to make false-marzipan topping. Add confectioner's sugar to taste to the mashed potatoes. Finally, a half teaspoon of almond flavoring. Beat well.

• To dry icing and frosting on hot muggy days, put the cake in the refrigerator for a few minutes. This will set the icing and keep it from running.

• If your frosting or icing dried before you sprinkled on the shredded coconut, moisten the coconut with a little milk.

• If you sprinkle a piece of waxed paper with confectioner's sugar, the paper will not stick to cake frosting.

• If you dust your cakes with cornstarch before you spread the icing or frosting, it will adhere better.

• Boiled frosting will not sugar if you add one teaspoon of white vinegar...or a quarter teaspoon of cream of tartar...or one tablespoon of white corn syrup during the cooking process.

• Need a quick frosting? For loaf cakes, when you remove them from the oven, place a chocolate bar on the cake and let it melt. You can do the same thing for cupcakes. As you take them from the oven, top each with a piece of plain chocolate.

• Another quick frosting tip: Melt a cup of semisweet chocolate bits over boiling water. Add ½ cup of sour cream and a pinch of salt. Stir until smooth. For slightly more exotic taste, add a tablespoon of plain peanut butter.

Cookies

• You can cut chilled cookie dough very easily if you use a wire cheese slicer.

• For perfectly round chilled cookie dough, pack in empty frozen orange juice cans. When you are ready to use the dough, remove the bottom lid and use it to push out the dough—just enough for you to slice off one cookie at a time.

• To prevent your cookies from becoming too brown on the bottom, turn the cookie sheet upside down. Then put the cookies on the sheet. Bake them this way.

• When baking cookies of any type, remove them from the oven two minutes before you should. They will continue cooking but will not brown too much on the bottom.

• If you want a waffle design on your cookies, press a potato masher into the dough before baking.

• Meringue cookies baked on a sheet of paper will not stick if you put the paper on a damp towel before trying to remove the cookies.

• Having trouble transferring your cut-out cookies from the counter top to the baking sheet? Try this method: Place the dough on the prepared cookie sheet. Make your cut-outs. Lift the excess dough from the cookies—and pop into the oven.

• When icing a large batch of cookies, use a clean, narrow paint brush. You'll be surprised how quickly you will be done.

• If your favorite cookie recipe calls for shaping the dough into one inch balls, use a melon-baller. Perfect one inch balls!

• When rolling cookie dough, use powdered sugar instead of flour. This prevents the "tough" texture that comes from using flour.

• Baked cookies can be frozen.

• Apple slices in the cookie jar keep your homebaked cookies moist and flavorful.

• Cookies sticking to the pan? Oil the spatula for easy removal.

• When sending cookies through the mail, protect them by using a bed of popcorn.

• To keep your cookies crisp, place a piece of crushed tissue paper on the bottom of your cookie jar.

Pies

• Before you place a two-crust pie in the oven, pour a cup of ice water over the top and tilt so the water runs off. This gives you a crisp upper crust with a satin sheen.

• To cut down the time for preparing apples, quarter them first. This makes coring and paring faster.

• If you use carbonated water or half lemon juice and half water when making pie crust, it will be flakier than ever before.

• When making apple pies, cut the fruit in cubes rather than slices. The cubes give better support to the upper crust.

• Save yourself the trouble of washing an extra bowl. Prepare your crust right in the pie plate.

• When using frozen pies, place the pies on a cookie sheet that has been pre-heated in the oven. Then bake the pie according to directions. This will give a nice brown bottom crust. And for an extra treat, sprinkle a little sugar on the top crust before baking.

• To eliminate bottom crust shrinkage, cover the dough with a piece of waxed paper. Make the paper about two inches wider than the pie plate. Place dry beans on the waxed paper and then bake the dough as you would normally. The beans will weight the crust and keep it from shrinking.

• Fruit pies tend to produce a soggy bottom crust. To prevent this, brush the bottom crust with soft butter. Let the butter harden and then add your filling.

• For quick baking pumpkin pie, prepare the filling and keep the bowl or pot in warm water, stirring often, while you prepare the crust. Let the crust bake for ten minutes. Then add the warm filling and return to the oven for the final baking.

• To get at fresh pumpkin meat quickly, cut the pumpkin in half and remove the seeds and fiber. Place the halves on a cookie sheet, cut sides down. Place in a hot oven until the shells collapse. The pumpkin meat can then be scooped out easily.

• To keep fruit and berry pies from boiling over, try this: Soak a slice of white bread in hot water and squeeze. Place bits and pieces

23

of wet bread over the leaky places on your pie. Bake as you would normally. When the pie is done, just remove the crusts and discard.

• You can prepare pie crust dough in advance and freeze it.

• Pie crusts can be broiled if you wish. This method does, however, require careful watching.

• To keep fruit and berry pies from boiling over, insert pieces of uncooked macaroni, about two inches long, into the pie crust before baking. The juice will bubble up the macaroni and not down onto your oven.

• After you make pie dough, let it rest for ten or fifteen minutes before you roll it out. The crust will be flakier if you do.

• Like that old-fashioned treat—grape pie? Put the skins through your food processor before adding them to the pulp. You get a thicker, tastier filling this way.

• Many bakers claim pie crusts come out flakier if the dough is molded around the pie plate which has been turned upside down.

• You can catch the juicy overflow from fruit and berry pies if you put the pie plates on a cookie sheet while baking.

• To keep meringue from shrinking, spread the egg white over the entire top of the pie. There should be no open spaces showing.

• You get more meringue if you add one tablespoon of cold water for every egg white you use. And there is no change in flavor.

• To keep the top crust from breaking as you transfer from the board to the pie, coat your rolling pin with flour.

• If you want to prevent the edges of your pies from burning, ring the pie with a strip of damp white cloth.

• Tired of soggy undercrusts? Before adding the filling, place the pieplate, lined with the unbaked crust, in your oven. Turn the temperature to the highest setting and bake for ten minutes. This will not bake crust, it will just set it. After you do this, add the filling and bake the pie at the recommended temperature.

• It will be easy to remember what kind of fruit pie you have in your freezer if you cut the initial of the fruit in the top crust. A for apple, P for peach.

• To keep the juice of fruit pies from leaking, make your top crust large and put it on loosely.

• For an extra sweet, flaky crust, spread your pastry board with powdered sugar rather than flour.

• You can get a better crust by using whole-wheat flour and butter or vegetable shortening instead of lard.

• Allow your pie dough to rest for fifteen minutes in the refrigerator before you roll it out.

- Before cutting a pie, dip your knife in cold water. This will prevent any sticking.
- Allow a baked pastry shell to cool thoroughly before you add the filling.
- To keep a lemon chiffon pie from falling, add a teaspoon of baking powder to the filling recipe.
- Always heat milk to the boiling point before mixing with the eggs for custard pie. This prevents the bottom crust from getting soggy.
- To cut lattice strips for fruit pies, use pinking shears dipped in flour.

Breads, Biscuits, Doughnuts

- Hot freshly baked bread slices quite easily if you run the blade of the knife through a flame first.
- For crisp, flaky biscuits, roll the dough and then fold into the desired size.
- Quick corn bread can be made if you spread the batter on your waffle iron.
- Your dough will stay at an even temperature when you are making yeast rolls if you keep the bowl on a warming tray set for medium heat.
- If you like old-fashioned sour-dough biscuits, they can be made in a hurry with commercial buttermilk biscuit dough. Dissolve one cake of yeast in warm milk and add to the commercial dough. Roll the dough out and cut into the desired size. Bake according to package directions. The secret is not to make the biscuits too thin—and let the dough sit for several hours in a warm place before you roll out the biscuits.
- When kneading bread dough, put it in a large plastic bag. This way, you can push and pull and pat and poke without doing damage to the dough itself.
- Yesterday's raised doughnuts will taste freshed baked if you warm them on a cookie sheet in your oven. Set the temperature between 275-300°F.
- To save cleaning a bowl, melt chocolate in its foil wrapper. You can also line your double boiler with aluminum foil.
- Save the wrappers from butter and margarine. Store them in your freezer. These wrappers have just enough grease on them to make greasing cake tins a snap.
- Baking is easier when you prepare ahead. When you cut liners for your cake pans, don't stop at one or two. Cut several and store

them in the cardboard tube from a roll of paper towels.

• Filled dough cakes are easier to cut if you use a piece of nylon thread. Slip the thread under the cake, pull the ends together and down. This gives you a clean slice and the filling stays in the cake.

• You can store poppy seed for up to six months by using this method: For each pound of poppy seed, add one cup of white sugar. The seeds will not become bitter or rancid.

• To thaw frozen bread or rolls quickly, place in 325°F oven for five minutes. (And bread should be stored in the freezer until ready for use. It keeps fresher longer.)

• To soften stalish bread, wrap in damp paper toweling and then aluminum foil. Place in 300°F oven for fifteen minutes.

• If you have more time, wrap the bread in a damp towel and place in the refrigerator overnight. The next day remove the towel and pop the bread into a moderate (300°F) oven for five minutes. This method gives the bread a fresh-baked taste.

• For peanut butter and jelly fans: Peanut butter tears fresh bread. To avoid this, place the bread slices in your freezer until hard. Spread the peanut butter. The sandwich will thaw out again in less than half an hour.

• For instant croutons, toast the heels of stale bread. Rub the inner side with a slice of cut garlic. Spread butter on each slice and cut into small squares. Store in a plastic bag in your freezer. When you need them, pop into a slow oven (250°F) for five minutes. Quick thaw and crisp taste!

• Never throw out the plastic bread wrappers. Turn them inside out and wash them thoroughly. Hang outside to dry. These wrappers make super storage bags.

• Make your own bread crumbs. Grate the slices in your blender.

• For instant casserole topping, take several cups of bread crumbs, add a tablespoon of melted butter or margarine for each cup, and a tablespoon of Parmesan cheese for each cup of crumbs. Blend the mixture thoroughly. Place on freezer paper and pat into a loaf. Wrap and store in your freezer. When preparing a casserole, just slice off the amount of topping you need. It will thaw by the time you finish the casserole.

GENERAL KITCHEN HINTS AND TIPS

• Save those egg shells. They are excellent for cleaning stained bottles and jars. Crush a handful, put them in the jar, add a little soap and water, and swish around.

• Keep a clean powder puff in your flour canister. It's just great for dusting pastry pans without wasting flour.

• Need really dry jars and bottles for storage? Place a cube of sugar in the container after washing. The sugar will absorb the moisture.

• When measuring molasses, honey or any sticky substance, coat the measuring spoon or cup with salad oil first. The sticky stuff will slide right out.

• Need to measure solid shortening in a hurry? Use a standard ice cream scoop; a ball of shortening is a quarter of a cup.

• Need cracked ice? Save milk or fruit juice cartons. Rinse them out. Fill with water and freeze. When you want the cracked ice, take the carton and slam it hard against something solid. Presto, slivered ice that slides out of the carton opening very easily.

• No more boil-overs if you add a lump of margarine or a tablespoon of oil to the cooking water.

• To slice sticky foods like raisins and dates, drop them into a paper bag of flour and shake. For marshmallows, freeze them first and then cut them.

• Most recipes call for salt AND pepper usually in a ratio of three to one. To save time, mix your own in a jar. For every tablespoon of salt, add a teaspoon of pepper. When you need ¾ teaspoon of salt and a ¼ teaspoon of pepper, just measure out a teaspoon of your mixture.

• The most frequently used temperature for your oven is 350°F. Mark that setting with a dab of red nail polish or paint. No more squinting at those tiny numbers.

• When doubling a recipe, increase the salt by one half only.

• Forget about those recipe instructions that read, "Chop very fine." Just grate—it will come out fine.

• For kitchen grease fires, pour on baking soda or salt.

• When opening cans of undiluted soup or tomato paste, remove the upper lid. Hold the can upside down over a pot or bowl and puncture the bottom. The contents will slide right out.

• An empty Worcestershire or soy sauce bottle makes a great vinegar dispenser for your table. Pry the plastic cap off gently. Rinse out the bottle and fill with vinegar.

KITCHEN SPACE MAKERS

• Making salad for a mob? Use the vegetable crisper of your refrigerator as a giant salad bowl. Keeps the salad crisp until serving time, too.

• Need an ice tub for a big party? Use your top-loading washing machine as a cooler.

• For more work space than you have, place a large cutting board across an open drawer.

KITCHEN BUDGET STRETCHERS

• In this day and age, the average family's grocery bill runs a close second to the cost of home heating oil. After each trip to the supermarket, we all gaze at the register tape looking for ways to cut back without sacrificing quality or quantity. There is a way! Avoid those fancy labels. Certain foods, no matter what the label reads, have the same chemical composition. For example, sodium chloride otherwise known as table salt. Whether you buy a nationally advertised brand, a store brand, or the increasingly more popular generic brand, you get sodium chloride. Not even a chemist could tell which was which.

There are a number of foods that are like salt. By selecting the store or even the generic brand, you save money without sacrificing quality or quantity. Here is a list of such products:

Baking powder	Honey
Baking soda	Molasses
Bread crumbs (unflavored)	Powdered milk
Cooking oils (except olive)	Nuts (except "mixed")
Corn starch	Extracts and flavorings
Dried fruits (raisins, dates)	Salt
Lemon juice	Spices and herbs
Lime juice	Sugar (all forms)
Vinegar	

CORRECTING COOKING CALAMITIES

We all goof in the kitchen occasionally. Frustrating and annoying? Yes, of course. But it is not a total loss. Relax. Many cooking errors can be corrected:

Wilted vegetables: Pick off any brown or blemished edges. Sprinkle with cool water and wrap in a dry towel. Refrigerate the vegetable for an hour or so.

Too sweet: Add salt, a very little at a time. For a main dish or a vegetable, you can add cider vinegar...again, a little at a time.

Too salty: For soup and stew, add sliced raw potatoes. When they absorb the excess salt, discard them. You can also add cider vinegar to overly salty soups and stews. Adding sugar, a bit at a time, will cut the salty taste.

To prevent salty mistakes: Add the salt to soups and stews at the beginning, to vegetables while they are cooking and to meats at the end of the cooking process.

CHAPTER 2
LAUNDRY

Oh, those washday blues. There's got to be an easier way! You bet there is! The biggest error we make on washdays is to ignore directions. Today, clothing, by law, must be labeled as to garment content and laundering requirements. Take time out to read those labels. And do the reading before you buy the item. If the label reads, "Dry Clean Only," and you don't want the hassle and expense, then don't buy that garment. Clothing that calls for dry cleaning cannot be safely washed at home.

When an item is machine washable, follow the manufacturer's directions as to temperature, setting, cycle and so forth.

Another thing we often ignore are the instructions on the various laundry products we use. So many of us assume if the instructions are, "Use half a cup," a full cup will do the job twice as well. Noooo . . .just the opposite. Modern-day laundry products are precision formulated. By using more than is recommended, you throw the formula out of whack. The laundry product does not give the expected results. Honest!

The general rules of laundering apply to ironing as well. If the garment label reads, "Cool setting," that's the temperature you use. Using a higher setting can ruin a garment beyond repair.

But enough. Clothing care, in all forms, can be a drag. Fortunately, there are many ways to take some of the sting out.

Stain Removal

If washing were just a matter of tossing dirty clothes in the machine and pushing a few buttons, we'd have very little to bother about. It's not, though. Getting the family clothes clean usually means stain removal first. Here are suggestions that really work for removing the more common stains:

Alcoholic Beverages: For freshly made stains, soak in cold water and then sponge with liquid detergent. Rinse in water to which a few drops of vinegar have been added. Wash in the normal manner. If the stain is still there, repeat the above procedure, using a sponging solution of one part alcohol and one part water. If the stain is still there, again, repeat the above procedure using a sponging solution of pure rubbing alcohol. Most alcohol stains will, however, disappear with a cold water soaking and a wash in the usual manner. Stains that have set, i.e., those already dry, should be spotted with rubbing alcohol and then washed in the usual manner. When working with acetate fabrics, use a solution of one part alcohol to two parts water.

Antiperspirants: Sponge the stained area with a mixture of detergent and warm water...or sponge with straight ammonia. For stains on silk and wool garments, use a solution of one part water to one part ammonia.

Beer: Sponge the soiled area with cold, clear water.

Bird Droppings: Add a handful of baking soda and one tablespoon of any soapless detergent to a half bucket of warm water. Scrub the stain with this solution. Rinse and wash as you usually would.

Bleach: For emergencies, cover the spots with a felt tip pen of approximately the same color. Black shoe dye works very well on black garments.

Blood (Animal and Human): Cover the area with a commercial meat tenderizer. Drip on enough cold water to make a paste. Wait fifteen to thirty minutes and rinse the garment in cool water...or you can rub the stained area with an ice cube. Hold a washcloth under the stain and rub briskly with the ice cube. The blood will run through to the cloth.

Butter and Margarine: When the stain is on white cotton or linen garments, wet them thoroughly. Apply a small amount of household scouring powder (a brand with bleach) and scrub with a brush. Let the garment set until the stains are gone. Wash as usual.

Candle Wax: Scrape off as much as you can with a dull knife. Place the stained area between two pieces of white tissue and press with a warm iron. Any remaining wax can be sponged off with a grease solvent.

Carbon Paper: Sponge area with a commercial dry cleaning fluid.

Catsup: Sponge with cool water and let set for thirty minutes. Work a detergent into the stain and rinse as you would normally. This method also works for chili sauce.

Chewing Gum: Put the garment in a plastic bag and freeze it. The hardened gum will flick right off...or you can loosen the gum by soaking the garment in white vinegar...or rub the stained area with egg white before washing.

Chocolate: Work glycerin into the stain and rinse thoroughly in plain water. Several applications may be needed.

Cod Liver Oil: Apply a solution of one part detergent and one part banana oil. Rub this into the stain and then wash as usual. If the spot remains, dab on a bit of hydrogen peroxide. For materials that cannot be washed, place a piece of soft cloth under the stain and sponge with denatured alcohol.

Coffee: Sponge with Borax and warm water...or soak overnight in a large pan of strong vinegar water. Dry in the sun while dripping wet. Wash as usual...or use commercial coffee pot cleaners, but follow the package directions...or if chlorine bleach safe, use a household bleach.

Cosmetics: Sponge with a sudsy detergent solution. Repeat this procedure until stain is gone. Let the garment dry between applications. If the cosmetic has a grease base, see below under grease.

Egg: Never use hot water as this will cause the stain to set. If the stain is dry, scrape off as much as possible and then sponge with cold water. Work detergent into the spot and wash as usual.

Fruit and Berries: Stretch the stained area over a bowl. Pour boiling water on the stain from a height of several feet. If the stain persists, rub it with glycerin first and then repeat the above instructions...or instead of glycerin, sponge the stain with hydrogen peroxide or lemon juice. For fabrics that cannot be washed in hot water, soak in cold water and rub glycerin into the fabric. Let it remain for several hours. Rinse thoroughly in water to which a few drops of white vinegar have been added. Wash as you would normally.

Glue: Apply nailpolish remover on the opposite side of the fabric. Peel off the glue.

Grass: Cover the stain with molasses and leave it on for several hours. Wash the garment in warm, soapy water...or work detergent into the stain and wash using the recommended bleach. If the stain is still there, let the item dry. Sponge the stain with rubbing alcohol, for colored fabrics, use a solution of one part water to one part rubbing alcohol.

Gravy: Soak in cold water and then wash as usual.

Grease: Rub detergent into the stain and rinse in hot water...or spot the stain with a commercial grease solvent mixed with talcum powder. Let the mixture dry and brush it off...or cover the spot with white flour. Fold a white paper towel or napkin several times to make a pad. Place this over the flour-covered stain and iron. The pad will absorb the grease. For non-iron fabrics, spot the stain with a solution of two tablespoons of washing soda mixed in a cup of warm water. Let it set for five minutes. Rinse. You can also rub grease stains with a cake of dry soap and then wash the garment in warm, soapy water. When you have a grease spot on a suede garment, sponge it with white vinegar or club soda. You can restore the nap with a suede brush. On double knit fabrics, sponge the stains with plain club soda.

Ice Cream: This is a case of fighting fat with fat. Rub the stain with a small amount of shortening and then wash the garment in hot water using a detergent.

Ink (Ballpoint): This can be a tough stain and requires experimentation. First, try using an eraser designed for ballpoint pens. Some ballpoint inks will wash right out. Mark an inconspicious part of the garment with the same type of pen and then rinse with warm water. No luck? Spot the stain with denatured alcohol or petroleum jelly and soak in a detergent solution. Wash normally. You can also saturate the stain with hairspray and then scrub hard. Cuticle remover will take off ballpoint ink stains from leather garments. For regular, **liquid ink**, cover the stain with a paste of milk and cornmeal. Allow to stand for a few hours and then brush off. . .or sprinkle the stain with table salt. . .or run cold water through the stain until the water is clear. Wash, using the recommended bleach. . .or soak in a solution of one part alcohol and two parts water. . .or make a thick paste of baking soda and water. Cover the stain and hold the spotted area over a pot of boiling water. Wash as you would normally.

Iodine: Soak the garment in cold water and then wash as you would normally. . .or cover the stain with white ink and then wash. . .or sponge the spot with plain ammonia and then wash.

Jam and Jelly: Soak in a solution of one ounce washing soda to two cups of warm water. Wash as you would normally.

Lipstick: Rub the stain with petroleum jelly and then wash in hot, soapy water. . .or rub the stain with a slice of white bread and brush away the crumbs. . .or place a white towel under the spot and sponge thoroughly with a thick mixture of powdered soap and water. Wash as you would normally. . .or saturate white material with full-strength lemon juice and for colored fabrics, diluted lemon juice. . .or sponge the stain with glycerin and let it set. Where safe for the fabric, rubbing alcohol or hydrogen peroxide can be sponged on the stain.

Mercurochrome: Soak the garment in a solution of four tablespoons of ammonia and a quart of water. . .when safe for the fabric, sponge the spot with rubbing alcohol. . .if the spot is stubborn, place a pad soaked with alcohol over the spot and leave it there until the stain is gone. Keep the pad damp.

Mold and Mildew: Rub the stain with a mixture of table salt and lemon juice. Place the garment in the sun. . .or soak the garment

33

overnight in sour milk. Rinse and dry in the sun...or treat stains with bleach appropriate to fabric. On leather, sponge the stain away with a solution of one part rubbing alcohol to one part water.

Mud: Let it dry first. This is important. Then brush away as much as you can. Soak in cold water and wash as you would normally. If the spot remains, sponge with denatured alcohol and wash again. You can also remove mud spots by rubbing them with raw potato.

Mustard: On washable fabrics, rub the stain with glycerin. Wash the garment in detergent...or rub detergent into the stain before washing.

Nailpolish: Apply nailpolish remover to the back of the stain. Before using the remover, test on an inconspicious spot to make sure the remover will not damage the fabric.

Paint: Treat these stains before the paint dries. For an oil-based paint, sponge the fabric with turpentine and then wash. Use a bleach if this is recommended. If the stains are from a water-based paint, sponge with a liquid detergent and wash. In either case, if the stains are still visible, soak the garment overnight in a strong detergent solution.

Pencil: Just erase them away!

Perspiration and Sweat: Sponge fresh stains with ammonia and the older ones with white vinegar. Rinse and wash as you would normally. Washable clothes can also be soaked in a strong solution of table salt and water...or apply a thick paste of baking soda and water to the stained area. Leave for about fifteen minutes and wash the garment as you would normally.

Ring Around the Collar: One of the easiest ways is to cover the dirty ring with plain chalk, the kind you can buy in any dime store. Leave the shirts overnight and wash as you would normally. You can also apply a paste of white vinegar and baking soda...or rub a little ordinary shampoo into the collar before washing.

Rust: Hold the stained area over a pot of boiling water and squeeze fresh lemon juice over the spot...or squeeze lemon juice over the spot, sprinkle on some salt, and place the garment in the sun...or, on white washables, cover the stains with cream of tartar and pour hot water over the stained areas. Wash as you would normally.

Salt Water: Sponge stain with warm water to dissolve the salt. If necessary, sponge stain again, this time with rubbing alcohol. Wash as you would normally.

Scorch Marks: Rinse the fabric in cold water immediately and sponge with washing soda and water. On white fabrics, sponge the marks with hydrogen peroxide. For linen and cotton, dampen a

34

cloth with hydrogen peroxide, place over the mark, and run a warm iron over the cloth. . .or dampen the mark and sprinkle corn starch over it. Allow the piece to dry and brush away the corn starch. . .or rub raw onion over the mark and then soak in cold water.

Shoe Polish: Where safe for the fabric, sponge the stain with rubbing alcohol. . .or work glycerin or mineral oil into the fabric and then use cleaning fluid.

Soot: Go over the spots with an art gum eraser and brush away the crumbs and the dirt.

Spaghetti: Sponge the stain with lemon juice and rinse. . .or go over the spot with a damp sponge and apply liquid bleach where safe for the fabric.

Tar: Scrape off as much as you can with a dull knife. Sponge the area with turpentine and trichloroethlene. . .or rub kerosene into the spot and then wash with detergent. Because kerosene does affect the color of most fabrics, test first on an inconspicuous spot.

Tea: Sponge with a solution of washing soda and water. . .use a commercial coffee pot cleaner. . .or pour boiling water over the stain. . .or sponge with hydrogen peroxide.

Tobacco: Sponge the spot with rubbing alcohol. If you cannot use alcohol on the fabric, follow the instructions for non-alcoholic removal of grass stains.

Urine (Animal and Human): Sponge with warm water and then apply a solution of one tablespoon of white vinegar to two cups of water.

Vomit: Sponge the area with washing soda and water. Rinse garment in warm water to which vinegar has been added and then wash as you would normally.

Water: If you rub a silver spoon over water spots on fabric, they will disappear.

Wine: For red wines, sprinkle the stain with lots of table salt. Rinse and wash as you would normally. . .or hold the fabric over a bowl and pour boiling water on it until the stain disappears. . .or apply a paste of salt and lemon juice. Rinse and wash in soapy water. . .or dip the stained area in boiling milk.

Miscellaneous: Spots on white garments can be removed by rubbing gently with an emery board or fine sand paper.

Small spots, most of them, can be removed quickly with a cotton swab dipped in cleaning fluid.

Yellowed one hundred percent cotton garments can be snow white again if they are soaked in a solution of one gallon of hot water, one-half cup of electric dishwasher compound, and one-fourth cup of liquid bleach. The solution should be used in a plastic, enamel or stainless steel container ONLY.

A FINAL NOTE ON SPOT REMOVAL: Always read the garment cleaning instructions on the label before trying any of these suggestions. Make sure the formulas, solutions and compounds suggested are safe for the particular fabric. If you have any doubts but want to try anyway, test out the suggestions on an inconspicuous part of the garment first.

Washing

• To get dirty white socks really white, put a slice of fresh lemon in a pot of water and boil. Then add the socks and let them bubble away. (Do not use this method if the socks have elastic bands or if they are wool.)

• For towels and clothes that smell musty, add two teaspoons of baking soda to a quart of water and boil the items.

• When washing quilts and blankets prior to summer storage, add a quarter of a cup of your favorite cologne to the rinse water.

• For firm, stiff, professional-looking nurse's caps, wash them as you would normally. Then smooth them out on a flat surface and give them a coat of spray starch. When they are dry, peel them up. You avoid ironing; a quick touch is the most the caps will need.

• Stuff small items, like baby socks, and delicate items, like your favorite nightie, into a pillow case. This protects these items from loss or damage during washing. It also prevents your having to fish around in the machine looking for that little sock.

• For washable woolens, make sure the rinse water is the same temperature as the wash water. A sudden change in water temperature "shocks" the garments and they shrink.

• If you tie aprons strings, sashes, belts and what have you before washing, you can avoid tangled clothes at the end of the washing cycle.

• By adding a little household ammonia to the water, clothes soiled by perspiration will come out minus a telltale odor.

• If a sweater must be worn soon after washing, speed up the drying process, wrap the item in a towel and squeeze. Use several towels if necessary. The more water absorbed by the terry towel, the less that will have to evaporate for total drying.

• Tired of yellow-looking nylon clothes? Here's a trick that works: Mix one gallon of hot water, one half cup of dishwasher detergent, and one quarter cup of household bleach in a plastic, enamel or stainless steel bucket. Let the mix cool to room temperature and add

36

the nylon clothes for a thirty-minute soak. Rinse them in cool water to which a splash of white vinegar has been added. The vinegar will neutralize the bleach. This method is suitable for white nylon clothing only. Never wash nylon, no matter what the color in hot water. That will set the wrinkles.

• When washing fiberglass items, never put them in with wearing apparel. The minute glass slivers from the fiberglass will get into your clothes—and can that ever irritate even the toughest skin!

• For those loose-knit sweaters, wash them as you would normally. Roll the sweater in a towel or several towels to remove all excess moisture. Finally, toss the sweater in the air a dozen times or so. This loosens up the knit again and makes the sweater fluffy.

• Now that white gloves are coming back in style, how to keep them clean without much trouble? After washing them, smooth them out on a flat surface and apply a very thin coating of spray starch. The starch protects them from really tough stains.

• For tennis shoes—the white ones, of course—wash them weekly with your bath towels. The towels serve as buffing clothes. Hang them to dry by the tongues. And for extra protection, a thin coating of spray starch.

• Tired of bleach spills? With a sharp pointed object like an ice pick, make a small hole about an inch below the spout. This will allow you to add bleach in small doses, a few drops at a time.

• Using a commercial laundry but find hauling detergent and dry bleach with you a drag? Measure out the necessary amounts and put them into a sock, or socks.

• The best fabric softener around is plain white vinegar. By adding a quarter cup to your wash instead of commercial softener, you will not only get the same results, but you will also save money. And there is no vinegar odor to contend with. Vinegar also serves to neutralize soap and detergent residue.

• When you're out of liquid detergent and have to wash woolens, shampoo will give you the same results.

Rinsing

Like washing, there are a few tips for rinsing clothes:

• If you add a teaspoon of Epsom salts for each gallon of rinse water, bright colored clothes will be brighter and dark colored clothes will not run.

• For wool garments, a few tablespoons of glycerine, or creme hair rinse, added to the final rinse leaves them softer.

• Rinse linen items twice in hot water to make sure all the soap or

37

detergent is gone. Soap or detergent film is what causes linen to turn greyish looking.

• Plastic items like shower curtains or rubber pants will stay soft and pliable if you add two tablespoons of glycerine to the rinse water.

• A quarter cup of your favorite cologne will give your clothes a nice aroma. After shave lotion is nice for men's clothes, too.

• Head and neck scarfs look like new if you add two tablespoons of table salt to the final rinse.

• When planning to store woolens for the summer, add three or four mothballs to the final rinse.

• Rinse your wash-and-wear items in cool water to prevent wrinkles.

• Polished cotton really looks polished if you add a half packet of plain gelatin to the last rinse water.

• If you add a cup of black coffee to the final rinse for dark-colored clothing, lint will not stick...or you can add a half cup of white vinegar to the final rinse for the same result.

• One half cup of powdered milk added to the final rinse leaves fiberglass and synthetic fabric curtains looking bright and almost new. There is no chance of a sour-milk smell developing either.

Laundry Problem Solvers

No matter how easy anything becomes, there are always a few problems. Here are some solutions for the most common laundry crisis:

• White nylon won't yellow if you pre-soak in a baking soda solution.

• No lint on black clothes if you add white vinegar to the final rinse. And you can really lick the lint problem if you place a yard of nylon net in your dryer. The net catches the lint.

• Your favorite sweater shrunk! This may help: Soak the sweater in a mixture of tepid water and shampoo. The fibers may loosen enough for stretching and reshaping.

• Stiff chamois becomes soft again if soaked in a mixture of warm water and two tablespoons of olive oil.

• Cracked buttons and broken zippers can be prevented if you button buttons and zip zippers and turn the garments inside out before washing.

• Dingy white handkerchiefs come clean when soaked in a solution of cold water and a teaspoon of cream of tartar.

• Still using feather pillows? You can get them both clean and feathery this way: Check for any open or weak seams and put the pillow in a pillow case. Fill your washing machine with warm water and add two terry towels. Push the towels into the machine so that they are completely wet. Now add the pillow (for balance, you are better off washing two pillows at a time). Make sure the pillows are soaked. Put the machine on the gentle cycle. Halfway through, stop the machine and turn the pillows over. For drying, put the pillows in your dryer along with a clean tennis shoe. Expect the drying process to take about two hours. Now to fluff them up, set your dryer on air and let the pillows tumble for fifteen minutes.

• As for velvet, raise the nap first. This will remove the wrinkles. Put the garment, pile side up, over boiling water to which a bit of ammonia has been added. Let the garment hang-dry. Give the garment a final brisk brushing and iron lightly on the wrong side.

Washing Machine Tips

And finally, a few miscellaneous washing hints and tips...

• Less than great performance from a washing machine may not necessarily mean an expensive visit from a repairman. Try cleaning it first. Fill the machine with warm water and add a gallon of white vinegar. Put the machine through the entire cycle. The vinegar will flush away accumulated soap or detergent scum.

• Too many suds? Sprinkle plain table salt over them.

• Can't remember how to wash a garment once the instruction label fades? Keep a card file on each piece. Make notations like this, "Susie's green blouse, nylon, cool water..."

• After doing dark or bright colored clothes in your machine, run the washer through a suds and rinse cycle. This assures you that all the color residue is gone.

• The average commercial spot remover is two parts water to one part rubbing alcohol.

• When the lint around the filter of your dryer is damp, it usually means the outside vent is clogged. Fast action in the form of a cleaning will prevent a costly, inconvenient breakdown.

• The cheapest, safest and easiest bleach to use is plain lemon juice.

Drying

Now that your clothes are washed, it's time to dry them. Whether you use a dryer or Mother Nature in the form of the great outdoors, there are ways to make whole process easier—on you:

• Are your clothes coming out of your dryer very wrinkled? You

39

could be overdrying them. Set your dryer for a shorter cyle.

• Drying indoors without a dryer? An expansion rod with suction cups at each end makes a good drying rack when hung over the tub.

• Another way to expand your drying space is by using an old umbrella. The skeleton makes a good indoor drying rack.

Outdoor Drying

Outdoor drying is gaining in popularity. One thing, it's free. For another, clothes smell better when dried in the great outdoors. Here are a few tricks on out door drying:

• On cold days, if you wipe the line with vinegar, the clothes won't freeze to the line. And to protect your hands, put on a thin pair of woolen gloves. Over the woolen gloves, wear a pair of rubber ones.

• For circle or bias-cut skirts, hang them by the waistband.

• It is easier to hang sheets if you put the hems together. You can arrange for this even before washing. Either pin the hems together or sew tiny snaps at each corner. Close the snaps before washing.

• For a lot of wash to hang, pull your laundry basket in your child's wagon. . .or put the clothes in one of those heavy wire-mesh grocery carts.

• For drip-dry cottons, nylon and orlon garments, take a wire hanger and put the plastic cover used by dry cleaners over the hanger. Slip the garment over this. Hang the hanger on the line and secure with a piece of wire used to close loaves of bread.

• If you hang blue jeans by the pocket lining they will dry faster because the air can circulate more easily.

• Dark and brightly colored clothes should be hung inside out to prevent sun fading. Remember, the sun is a super bleaching agent.

• Clothes won't freeze on cold winter days if salt is added to the final rinse water.

• Are you one of the lucky ones who still has Grandma's old-fashioned curtain stretcher? Wonderful! Use it. When you pin on the curtains, give them a light coating of spray starch and no more ironing curtains! To avoid nicking your fingers while stretching curtains, push the material onto the pins with a fork. Curtain stretchers are also great for drying blankets. The pinholes will disappear if you rub them with your fingers.

• Watch your clothes pins though. If they get dirty, you can clean them by soaking them in a solution of water and bleach. Any rough spots on the pins can be sanded away.

Ironing

Now's the really hard part, the ironing. Fortunately, there are fewer and fewer fabrics on the market today that really require ironing. But for those that do, the chore can be made bearable.

• The first rule of ironing is never just iron. Do it while watching a television show or chatting with a friend. Gives yourself just enough of a distraction.

• And let Mother Nature sprinkle your clothes. Even if your clothes are dry at the end of the day, leave them on the line overnight. When you bring them in the next morning, you will find that the dew has dampened them just enough. Not ready to iron yet? That's fine, too. Put the damp clothes in a plastic bag and store them in the refrigerator until you are.

• For small or quick ironing jobs, no need to haul out the ironing board. Spread a terry towel along a countertop.

• If you spread aluminum foil between the padding and cover of your ironing board, the job will go much faster. The foil gets hot and reflects further heat through the cover.

• Out of spray starch but need some article of clothing to look particularly crisp? Place a sheet of waxed paper over the item and iron away.

• For really big ironing jobs, like tableclothes, pad your kitchen table with towels, cover with an old sheet, and secure with twine. Presto! the biggest ironing board you've ever seen.

• If you want to speed up your ironing, there's no need to press an entire shirt or blouse. Why iron the part that's going to be tucked in? It'll only get wrinkled again.

• Always iron cutwork, embroidery and other fine items wrong side up. As for doilies, why iron them at all? When they are washed and ready for drying, spread them out on a terry towel. Arrange them so that they have their original shape. Then give them a heavy dose of spray starch.

• Wash-and-wear garments should be pressed on the wrong side to prevent that telltale shine. This is also true for heavy cotton materials.

• Want to avoid curled shirt collars? Start at the point and iron toward the back—halfway. Do the other point the same manner. This will cause the fabric to "bunch" in the back and keep the points lying flat.

• Boxer shorts giving you a hassle? Try this: Pull one leg down inside of the other to get a "half pair" of shorts. Then iron on the wrong side. Unfold for that final whisk with the iron. This also works for slacks and pajama bottoms.

• Small items like handkerchiefs can be ironed in two and threes. The fabric is usually so thin that the heat penetrates. Damp handkerchiefs, guest towels and such also make good pressing clothes when ironing woolens.

• If you own a dress form AND a circular skirt, when you have to iron the skirt, put in on the form. Adjust the height to your ironing board—no more slipping and sliding with the skirt.

• A stiff, dampened toothbrush will let you open seams as you iron. As for tucks, iron them until they are dry. Slightly damp tucks pucker. For vertical tucks, iron lengthwise; for horizontal ones, iron from top to bottom.

• To protect fancy or heat-sensitive buttons while ironing, cover them with the bowl of a spoon.

• To keep pants looking a little cleaner a little longer, spray the seat and the knees with spray starch while ironing. This trick is especially good for children's clothing.

CHAPTER 3

LOOKING YOUR BEST

First impressions, we are told, are the most lasting. Therefore, we try to look our best at all times, but it is not always easy. Especially with the busy lives we lead today. With the following ideas, however, you can look your best no matter how busy you are. And the first step is organization:

Organizing Closets and Drawers

• By supplying a thick coat of floor or paste wax to the rods in your closets, you will find hangers slide back and forth more easily. And hang clothes open part toward the back. This makes taking several garments from the closet all at once that much easier.

• An old faded blouse makes an ideal cover for wearable garments you want to protect.

• Place strips of elastic tape on the inside of your drawers. Using thumb tacks, make loops. Now you can store small bottles of perfume, nail polish, and other odd items without having them drop out of sight under your clothes.

• Use cardboard boxes of various sizes to divide your drawers into neat compartments. Egg cartons make good storage places for jewelry.

• Those stepped plate holders sold in dime stores are perfect for storing handbags. Always store your bags with the handle out. This will keep the handle from getting crushed.

• When your closet is dark and gloomy even with the room light on, paint the interior with white enamel. When the room light is turned on and the closet door opened, the enamel paint will reflect the light. You'll be able to root around with better sight.

Shirts

• Wrap a not-too-often worn shirt in a sheet of waxed paper and seal the edges with a warm iron. Not only does this keep the shirt spotlessly clean, but it also prevents discoloration.

• While travelling, you can give your wash-and-wear shirts a washing. Wear the shirt into the shower and soap it down. Rinse it off as you rinse you. And because the collars and cuffs of wash-and-wear shirts tend to collect dirt, before you wash it rub these areas

43

with a dry bar of soap. Then work the soap in with your fingers.

• To keep shirts from bulging at the waist, hook a rubber band around the lowest button. Sew a small button inside the waist band of your skirt or pants. Wrap the other end of the rubber band around this button. The shirt (or blouse) stays tucked in where it belongs; the rubber band provides "give" whenever you raise your arms.

• If you put some sort of indelible ink on the collarbands of shirts with French cuffs, you will save time while dressing. No more rooting around to learn which shirts have French cuffs and which do not.

• Dirty French cuffs can be hidden quickly. Take out the links and bend the cuffs inward. Reinsert the links.

• Discolored shirt buttons can be restored to their original color if they are rubbed with an ink eraser.

• A too highly starched collar buttonhole can be loosened if you moisten the area with warm water.

• Fuzz around the shirt collar can be removed with an electric razor. This method does not damage the fabric.

Suits

• If pants are lined at the knees, they will never go baggy.

• When being fitted for a suit, make sure you fill the pockets with the stuff you usually carry. This way, the fit will be right.

• For quick pressing of a jacket, insert a rolling pin wrapped in a bath towel into the sleeves. Makes the whole job easier, and this method insures that there will be no crease in the sleeve.

• Loose buttons will stay put until they can be repaired if you wrap what's left of the thread with a thin strip of cellophane tape.

• For men who carry valuables in their inside breast pockets, add a small zipper. There's no chance the items will fall out. And a zipper certainly discourages pickpockets.

• Running out of hangers for pants? A towel bar on the inside of the closet door will serve as well.

• When pants become damp, a good, strong finger crease can save a pressing.

• Tired of shiny bottoms on woolen pants? When you have to do a lot of sitting, use a fabric covered seat pad. Extended sitting on leather or plastic causes the fabric to take on the shine.

• Tired of grabbing someone else's raincoat, or having them grab yours? Make some sort of distinctive mark on the inside of the yoke. Bright colored thread, indelible ink, nail polish. Almost anything will serve the purpose.

• Sweater pockets lined with cotton fabric will not stretch out.
• A stuck zipper can be opened if you run an ordinary Number Two pencil along it. . .or to prevent sticking in the first place, open the zipper and give it a thin coat of spray starch.
• When wearing a corsage, always remove any metal foil. The foil can leave a mark on clothing. Push a small piece of eraser on the pin.

Gloves

• Leather gloves are best washed in shampoo or soap containing lanolin. This restores the natural oils to the leather. Add a few drops of olive oil to the rinse water for doeskin, pigskin and chamois gloves. This insures that they will stay soft and pliant.
• Don't wring your leather gloves after washing. Lay them on a bath towel and reshape them. Then roll the towel up. This effectively removes excess water without damaging the shape.
• Store leather gloves in tissue paper so they can "breathe".
• Tired of mislaying your gloves? Or worse, losing just one? Sew small name tags on the inside. For leather gloves, you don't really need a tag, a marking pencil or indelible ink will do.
• Here's how to clean white kid gloves: Put them on your hands and dunk them in rubbing alcohol. Remove them carefully by rolling off rather than pulling. After drying is done, rub the gloves with egg white. Your white kid gloves will look brand new.
• White kid gloves can also have a dry cleaning of sorts. Put them on and rub moist bread crumbs or white corn meal all over. Remove by rolling down and buff the leather with a flannel cloth.
• Small spots can be removed from white kid gloves if you use an art gum eraser.
• You can dye your white kid gloves by soaking them in strong black coffee. Now you can get double wear out of them.

Hats

After years of neglect, this fashion accessory is back in style and so a few ideas on chapeau care:
• The leather sweatbands found on the inside of men's hats collect oil and dirt. From time to time, wipe off the bands with a damp cloth that has been rinsed in soapy water. By coating the band of a new hat with paraffin, you can keep the oil and dirt deposits to a minimum.
• For hats that have been mud stained, let the mud dry completely before brushing.

• Soot marks can be removed from a felt hat quite easily. Sprinkle table salt on the smudges. Remove the salt with a stiff brush. For light-colored felt hats, use a mixture of two tablespoons of cornmeal and a teaspoon of salt. Apply with a soft cloth. Use a stiff brush to rub away the cleaning mixture.

• For a really special cleaning, hold a felt hat upside down over a pan of boiling water for a second or two. Brush the hat with the nap and not against.

• You can write your name and address in indelible ink on the inside of the leather sweatband. Should you forget your chapeau, chances are it will come back to you.

• Rain-spotted felt hats can be restored if you rub the spots with a wad of tissue paper. Use a circular motion.

• Straw hats look bright and new when given a coat of ordinary hair spray.

• Need racks for all those fashionable hats you are acquiring? Empty, one pound coffee cans, covered or uncovered, make perfect ones.

Hosiery

• Keep a pair of thin nylon gloves with your hoisery. This will remind you to wear gloves while putting on your stockings. Covered hands prevent snags and runs.

• After rinsing and hanging hoisery to dry, give them a thin coating of spray starch. This serves as a protective shield against snags and runs but does affect the color.

• To add to the life of your hosiery, dunk a new pair in water. Don't rinse or squeeze them. Place them in a plastic bag in your freezer. When the stockings are frozen, let them thaw and dry. From then on, wash them in cold water. After rinsing, let them soak in a bowl of ice water until the ice is melted. Then hang to dry. This constant chilly treatment strengthens the nylon threads.

• Unexpected runs can be stopped if you apply a dab of clear nailpolish . . . or if you gently rub a bar of dry soap over the top of the run.

• When you find yourself with a pile of mismatched stockings, make them all one color. Place in a pot with enough water to cover and let them boil gently for fifteen minutes. When they are cool enough to handle, hang your stockings to dry.

Handbags

• To keep the metal trim on your bags from tarnishing, apply a coat of clear nail polish.

• When the handle of your favorite bag wears out, and it is usually the first part to go, having it replaced can be difficult. Often it is hard, if not impossible, to match the new handle material to the old. Instead of tossing the bag out, replace the handle with an inexpensive chain necklace from the dime store. Select a good, heavy type and—presto!! Your bag is back in service.

Handbag organization is a constant struggle. Here are a few ideas to help you win the battle of the messy bag:

• An empty lipstick tube makes a great holder for pins and paper clips that you may want to carry with you.

• You will always have your subway tokens near at hand if you string them on a large safety pin and hook the pin to the inside lining of your purse.

• And tired of hunting for your keys? Run a large, heavy duty type paper clip through your key ring. Then hook the paper clip through the hole of the zipper. For bags without an inner zipper compartment, use a large safety pin and hook it to the inside lining of your bag.

Shoes

• After polishing white shoes, make sure the polish is completely dry. Then rub the shoes with waxed paper. This prevents the polish from rubbing off on dark clothing. And it is just perfect for baby shoes. Another method that works quite well is to apply a coat of clear shoe polish after the white liquid polish has dried thoroughly.

• Sanding the soles of brand new shoes will keep you from slipping and sliding all over the place.

• The new fashionable wooden-heeled shoes respond very well to treatment with clear furniture wax. And to keep them from getting all knicked and scratched, coat them with clear nail polish when brand new.

• Patent leather shoes of any color are best polished with petroleum jelly or castor oil. Yes, that old-fashioned method really works because it keeps the leather from drying out and cracking. Orange juice also makes patent leather gleam.

• More on patent leather shoes. The original luster can be restored when you apply a thick layer of soapsuds to the shoes. Rub in with a damp sponge. Wipe off the soap with a clean, damp sponge and polish with a dry soft cloth. A solution of white vinegar and warm water will remove spots from patent leather shoes. For badly scuffed patent leather shoes, give them a coat of black paste shoe polish. Rub the polish in and then coat the shoe with clear nail polish. Future polishing just requires another coat of the nail polish.

• India ink is a good way to hide scuffs and scratches on black shoes. When the ink dries, polish the shoes. No one, including you, will notice the "paint job".

• For a quick shoeshine, use this method. Go over the shoes with a dry cloth. Sprinkle a few drops of water on the shoes and buff to a high shine with a clean, dry cloth. If you really need a hurry-up shine, rub your shoes with the inside of a banana peel.

• Worn out terry cloth towels make super polishing clothes for shoes. So do old bits and pieces of carpeting. And for a really fantastic gloss, try using old nylon stockings!

• To keep the toes of your shoes from getting scuffed, apply a thin coat of shellac after each polishing.

• Shoe laces last longer and stay cleaner if you give them a coat of spray starch. On both sides, of course.

• White linen shoes meant to be dyed to match a particular outfit can be used again and again. Wipe off the original shade with a bleach and water mixture. Let the shoes dry thoroughly. Then dye again, according to package directions, to suit your needs.

• Shoe odor can be prevented and eliminated. To prevent this problem, put ordinary blotting paper in your shoes when not wearing them. The blotting paper absorbs the moisture from your feet which causes the odor in the first place.

• To get rid of the smell, saturate a ball of cotton with ordinary pine-scented household cleaner. One ball of cotton for each shoe. After you have placed the cotton in the shoes, put your footwear in a plastic bag and close it tightly. Leave them in a bag overnight.

• Scuffs and scratches on colored leather shoes can be covered with crayons. The kind you buy for kids. The jumbo box contains almost any shade of any color you will ever need.

• Rain-soaked shoes should be rubbed thoroughly with saddle soap while still wet. The application of saddle soap will keep them from becoming stiff. Dry away from direct heat—far away. And a good idea—hook your wet shoes, by the heels, over a chair rung. Not only will the shoes be out of the way, but the air will also be able to circulate freely around them.

• If you spray your new canvas shoes with fabric protector or even starch, they will last longer—and stay cleaner, too.

• You can clean the rope trim on shoes with rug shampoo. Use a stiff toothbrush to rub the shampoo in.

Ties and Belts

• The metal clips on bow ties will never tarnish or leave rust marks on shirts if you coat the clip with at least four coats of clear nail polish. Make sure one coat is completely dry before applying the next one. This same trick works for belt buckles, too.

• When the fabric wears off your belt buckle, coat exposed metal with a suitable shade of nail polish. Usually three coats does the job.

• Ties have that "just pressed" look if hung in the bathroom while someone takes a real steamy shower.

• You can make an inexpensive and practical tie rack for your closet. Insert two cup hooks either inside the closet door or on the closet wall. Stretch a heavy duty rubber band between the two hooks.

• To prevent steam creases on ties, insert a piece of cardboard cut to shape through the long end.

Underwear

• Your slip won't cling to your dress if you starch the slip ever so slightly. Another cling-free idea—you can draw out the electricity by running a wire coat hanger between your dress and nylon slip.

• Tired of slip and bra straps rolling down your shoulders? Sew one end of a small piece of cloth tape on the inside of your garments. The tape should be parallel with your shoulder. Sew snaps at the other end. When you dress, slip the tape under your straps and snap it closed.

• When a full slip wears out, cut the bottom half off. Stitch in a hem...presto! A camisole top to wear with slacks.

• To keep your bras in shape, don't hang them. Dry them flat with a rubber ball of appropriate size in each cup.

General Clothing Tips

• To insure that you don't lose a button while out, touch the threads lightly with clear nail polish.

• An unexpected spot on white fabric can be masked with baby powder.

• Hem creases will disappear if you saturate the material with white vinegar and then press with a warm iron.

Suede

Here are some ideas for the care of suede garments: Rub the garment lightly with fine sand paper and wipe with a cloth moistened in white vinegar...you can also remove dust with a vacuum cleaner. Use the upholstery brush attachment. To store suede garments without mildew worry, place a piece of chalk in the pocket. You can clean your suede clothes by rubbing them with a piece of stale bread. Brush away the crumbs with a soft brush. Old nylon stockings make ideal rubbing cloths for suede. Black suede can be renewed by wiping with a sponge dipped in strong black coffee. Wring the sponge before using it.

Eyeglasses

• Rubbing alcohol or ginger ale will dissolve sun tan oil that is on your specs.

• Tired of streaky eyeglasses? Use a drop of white vinegar, gin, or vodka on each lens and polish as usual.

• By applying a thin coat of soap to the lens and polishing until clear, you will waterproof your specs and keep them from fogging up when you go from the cold outdoors to the warm indoors.

Hair Care

To keep your crowning glory at its best, consider:

• For a longer lasting set, wrap lots of toilet tissue around your rollers and cover with a curler cap.

• Beer is a terrific setting lotion. When dry, it leaves no odor but gives your hair more body. Fill an empty spray bottle with beer so it is handy each time you do your hair.

• Other handy set aids—a teaspoon of sugar or plain gelatin dissolved in one cup of warm water. For a really firm set, use prepared gelatin. Use it as you would a setting gel. Witch hazel provides a good strong set, too.

• For a quick set, do your hair up in rollers or pins and cover your head with a warm, damp towel for a few minutes.

• One half cup of mayonnaise applied to dry, unwashed hair is a good conditioner. Cover your head with plastic and wait fifteen minutes. Rinse thoroughly and then shampoo as you would normally.

• A quarter of a teaspoon of olive or baby oil massaged into your hair and scalp is a great conditioner. Wrap your head in a towel and relax under your dryer for a while.

• Here's how to achieve truly shiny hair. After you have washed your hair, rub in two well-beaten egg yolks. Leave on for half an hour and then rinse off thoroughly with lukewarm to cold water.

• For terrific highlights, rinse your hair with chamomile tea.

• Blondes get the best results when they rinse their hair with water containing a tablespoon or two of lemon juice. Brunettes and red-heads should use apple cider vinegar in their shampoo rinse water...or they can use black coffee as their **final** rinse. What a shine the coffee gives!

• One tablespoon of salt mixed in with one half cup of cornmeal is a fine dry shampoo. Apply generously to hair and brush well. Baby powder or cornstarch also make good dry shampoos.

• To avoid messing your hairdo while trying on dresses, carry a shower cap in your purse. The ones given out by motels are great for this.

Fingernails

• To get more life from your emery boards, cut off the worn ends with a pair of nail scissors.

• The striking side of a match book makes a good emergency emery board.

• If you don't care for polish yet want your fingernails to look shiny, apply dry soap to each nail and buff. You can also use lemon peel for the same result.

• For a manicure soak dip your nails in a cup of warm water to which the juice of half lemon has been added.

• Nail polish will really dry if you dip your fingers in a bowl of ice water when the polish is partially dry. Holding your hands in the freezer will dry the polish fast, too.

• When you buy a new bottle of nail polish, coat the inside of the cover and the top with petroleum jelly. Never again will the top of a bottle of nail polish stick.

• To prevent nail polish from getting thick, store it in the refrigerator. If the polish is thick, place the bottle in a pan of boiling water for a few minutes. Loosen the cap first.

Skin Care

• You can get relief from sunburn if you apply apple cider vinegar...or pat the burn gently with a wet tea bag...or apply a paste of baking soda and water.

• Before swimming in salt or chlorine water, apply a dab of petroleum jelly to your eye lids and lashes. This will prevent that burning sensation.

• Petroleum jelly and baby oil are just great for removing eye makeup.

• Any and all common household oils such as sunflower, cod liver, corn, olive, make great conditioners for dry skin.

- Witch hazel can be used as an astringent for oily skin.
- Skin tip for your husband: Witch hazel is a soothing after shave lotion. And when he runs out of shaving cream, suggest he use your cold cream.
- Fond of avocados? Don't throw the skins away until you rub your elbows with them. Your elbows will lose that flakey look.
- Well-beaten egg whites applied to your face act as a deep cleansing agent. Avoid the under eye area.
- Need an inexpensive facial moisturizer? Wash your face completely. While wet, rub in a small amount of petroleum jelly. Splash water on your face until the oily look disappears. Pat your face dry.
- A product called Miracle Whip can do more than brighten your salads. It removes dead facial skin. Rub a small amount into your skin and let it dry. Massage your face vigorously with your fingertips. Rinse off with warm water and pat dry. Try this on your feet, knees, and elbows, too. Good-bye to dead skin.
- After washing your face, fill the basin with warm water and add some apple cider vinegar. Splash this on your face and let it dry without toweling. If you do this once a day, your face will achieve the correct acid balance.
- A paste made of oatmeal and water will firm up your face. Apply liberally to your face and rub in well. Allow it to dry. Rinse off with warm water.
- If you mix a teaspoon of sugar with soap lather, you will have cleansing grains you can use everyday.
- For a once a week deep pore cleansing, boil a quart of water. Remove from heat and add the juice of half a lemon and a handful of your favorite herbs. Cover your hair with a towel and hold it in place with a shower cap. Close your eyes and bend your face over the steaming bowl of herbs and lemon. Enjoy this for fifteen minutes. Keep your face about twelve inches from the steam. NOTE: This is a once-a-week treat.
- Facial blemishes dry up quickly if you dab them with lemon juice or apple cider vinegar.
- Fresh cold cucumbers applied to your eyelids get rid of redness and that tired look.
- For stay-proof makeup, try this: Before applying your makeup splash cold mineral water on your face and let it dry. Do up your face. Moisten a ball of cotton with the mineral water and dab it over your face. This will set the makeup.

Cosmetic Savers
- The scent of perfume will last longer if you apply a thin layer of

petroleum jelly to your skin and then the perfume. The petroleum jelly adds oil to your skin and oily skin holds perfume longer.

• When your lipstick breaks, don't throw it out. Insert a toothpick and heat until the lipstick melts enough to be pushed together again. Then put it in the refrigerator.

• If you cut your lipstick on the diagonal for a sharper point, don't throw the bits and pieces away. Save them in a shallow dish and apply them to your mouth with a lipstick brush.

Personal Care

• Straight lemon juice makes a quick emergency mouthwash and gargle.

• Brush your teeth with mashed strawberries for a good cleaning. Plain baking soda will remove stains from your teeth.

• Find commercial deodorants expensive these days? Here are recipes for both cream and liquid types: For cream deodorant, mix two teaspoons of baking soda, two teaspoons of petroleum jelly and two teaspoons of talcum powder. Heat the mixture in a double boiler until a smooth cream forms. Let it cool a bit and transfer to a jar with a tight lid. Apply as you would a commercial cream deodorant. For the liquid type, mix two tablespoons alum which you can buy at any drug store, with one pint of warm water. Stir well. You can add a few drops of your favorite cologne or after-shave lotion if you prefer a nice scent. Store this mixture in a spray bottle.

• For emergency lint removal, carry a plastic hair roller in your handbag. One of those fuzzy magnetic type rollers. It really does the trick. What's more, it is light to carry, takes up very little room in your bag, and can be rinsed out quickly.

• No more mistakes when buying wearing apparel. How many times have you bought a blouse, or some other garment, thinking it would go perfectly with an article home in your closet only to find it really doesn't? No need to carry all your clothes with you all the time. Whenever you're buying clothing, snip a small piece from an inside seam and staple it to a 3x5 card. Carry the card in your purse or wallet. The next time you spot a possible addition to your wardrobe, whip out your card and check.

JEWELRY – ITS CARE AND PROTECTION

Repairs on valuable jewelry, whether the worth is based on cold hard cash or on sweet sentiment, should always be made by a professional. You can, however, do much to insure repairs are kept to a minimum by caring for your pieces. When repairs are necessary, have them made at once. Broken jewelry has two disadvantages. You cannot wear the piece, and what's the fun of having something that you cannot enjoy? Second, a piece of good jewelry in need of fixing is worthless. Who today can afford that?

Cleaning Jewelry

Amber: Never put amber in water. Place a drop or two of OLIVE oil on a piece of cotton and rub the oil into the amber gently.

Amethysts, crystal, emeralds, rubies, sapphires, topazes, and turquoises: Add a tablespoon of ammonia to warm, soapy water. Scrub the stones gently using a baby's toothbrush. Rinse in clear, warm water. Place on a clean, lint-free cloth to dry.

Diamonds: Add a tablespoon of ammonia to hot, soapy water. Scrub well. Rinse in hot, clear water. Dip the stones into alcohol and let them dry on a clean, lint-free cloth.

• For a quick cleaning, put a little toothpaste or powder on a small brush. Scrub the stones and rinse in hot water. Dry as above.

• For extra sparkle, let your diamond soak in plain seltzer water for ten to fifteen minutes. Dry on a clean, lint-free cloth.

Ivory: Use plain denatured rubbing alcohol and a soft cotton cloth or swab. Rub clean. Do not dilute the solution. Never use water or any type of paste. These will change the shape of the ivory pieces. After the cleaning, dry with a clean, lint-free cloth. For an extra high shine, apply a drop of lemon oil.

Jade, Jet and Mother-of-Pearl: Use warm, soapy water. Pat dry with a clean lint-free towel. Do not rub and never soak these stones.

Opals: Never use water. These stones are not only delicate, but they are also extremely porous. Clean them by rubbing a drop of lightweight oil into them (glycerine is ideal). Then polish the opals gently with a clean, lint-free cloth.

Pearls: Rub them often with a clean, lint-free cloth. To really clean them, wear them as often as possible. Pearls absorb the natural oils of your skin and enhance the shine. Between wearings, store your pearls in rice.

Restringing Tips

• Extremely valuable beads should always be restrung professionally at least once a year. For beads of nominal value, use the finest fishing line you can buy at your local sporting goods store. Fine fishing line is tough—you will not have to use a needle.

• To keep beads of graduated size in order, take a long piece of adhesive tape. Lay it sticky side up. If the ends curl, hold them down with small pieces of adhesive. Place the beads along the tape in size order.

Unknotting Chains

• Take a drop or two of salad oil. Dip the knotted portion into the oil. Using two straight pins, unwork the knot. Rinse the oiled section in ammonia.

Cleaning Custom Jewelry (Except Plastic Pieces)

• Put the pieces in a bowl. Pour in enough rubbing alcohol to cover them. Let them soak for five minutes. Rinse in warm water and dry with a clean, lint-free towel.

• Dull rhinestone pieces will shine if soaked in detergent for about fifteen minutes. Rinse in warm water and rub dry with a clean flannel cloth. Or...

• Dunk metal pieces in a small bowl filled with warm water and detergent. Rinse in warm water and dry with a clean flannel cloth.

• A small piece of white chalk placed in your custom jewelry box will keep the pieces from tarnishing.

Storing Jewelry

• To keep your favorite pins and brooches within easy reach—display them! Take an old picture frame and remove the glass. Cover the backing with a piece of velvet. Stick your pins and brooches on and hang the frame in a convenient spot. Not only are your favorite pieces always handy, but your jewelry box is less cluttered.

Removing Tight Rings

• Soak your hand in ice-cold soapsuds. Rub the suds on your finger until the ring slips off—which it will do soon.

Protecting Your Jewelry

• When wearing a pin or brooch, take a piece of adhesive tape and stick it behind the lapel or on the inside of your dress. Stick the pin through both the fabric and the tape. Lock the safety catch. There is no chance of your brooch or pin becoming undone and falling off.

• For those of you who wear eyeglasses **and rings**, when washing your hands, slip the rings onto the earpiece of your specs. No more leaving your prized rings on the shelf of some washroom.

• If you wear screw-back earrings, when you remove one—to use the telephone, for instance—never put the earring down. Screw it to your watchband.

CHAPTER 4

SEWING, MENDING AND DARNING

A stitch in time saves nine we are told. Here's how to save six, seven, eight, let alone nine, stitches. And when you have more than nine stitches, how to make the process go faster.

Buttons

• When sewing on buttons with four holes, sew two holes on, knot the thread and sew the next two holes. When the thread breaks on one pair of holes, the other will still be secure. The result—fewer lost buttons—and faster mending.

• Dental floss or elastic thread is very practical for buttons. There is a certain amount of "give" which means the buttons stay on longer. And the "give" is useful for those who put on a few extra pounds—the buttons won't pop off.

• When you have trouble removing buttons, slip a comb under the button and take it off with a single-edged razor blade.

• Making straight buttonholes in heavy fabric can be a chore. To make it easier, lay the buttonhole over a piece of soap. Make the buttonhole with a single-edged razor blade.

• To line up snaps exactly, sew the pointed snap on first. Mark the point with a piece of chalk and press against the opposite side of the garment. There you have the mark for the other half of the snap.

• When you make your own buttons from sheer fabric, the metal often shows through. To prevent this, cover the button with a circle of mending tape first and then the fabric of your choice. The buttons last longer, too.

• When sewing on buttons, the job goes faster if you quadruple the thread, rather than just doubling it.

• To make sweater buttons even more secure, don't knot the thread in the usual way. When you start, leave about an inch of thread. When you finish, cut the thread so you have another inch. Tie the two ends together.

• A fine-toothed comb makes sewing buttons on heavy fabric easier. Place the comb between the button and the material. Push the needle through the teeth. The thread stays equal for each stitch and you do not sew the button on too tightly.

- To really secure buttons on children's clothing, sew a strip of strong cotton tape on the garment behind the buttons. Then secure the buttons.
- You can make pearlized buttons match the garment if you boil them for ten or fifteen minutes in a concentrated dye solution of the desired color.
- When you want buttons to stay in a straight line while you are sewing them on, line them up and hold them in place with a strip of cellophane tape. You can sew right through the tape and pull it off when you are done.
- To keep unsewn buttonholes from unraveling while you are working on them, spray them with starch.

Button Keeping

- To keep your button box neat and organized, store matching buttons between two strips of cellophane tape. As you need a button or two, you can snip off the tape.
- Empty plastic pill bottles from the drug store are great for storing buttons without confusion. And the child-proof safety lids insure that your little ones will not swallow a button for a snack.

Sewing Savers

- If rough skin causes tiny snags while you are doing fine sewing, wear a pair of rubber surgical gloves. They are available at any drug store.
- The cuffs from worn out socks can be used to replace worn sweater cuffs.
- Before working on light-colored fabrics, dust your hands with corn starch. The corn starch will absorb any perspiration from your hands and keep the fabric clean.
- If you pad the pockets of work pants with a thin piece of foam rubber sponge, the pockets will be less likely to develop holes.
- When you reverse shirt collars or cuffs, spray them liberally with spray starch first. They will be much easier to work with.
- When darning socks, make your stitches loose. During washing, the yarn will shrink making the darn almost invisible. And those who wear the sock will find less irritation from the thread.
- When mending the finger in a glove, use a marble as your darning egg. For the darning egg you use for socks, paint one side with a dark color paint and the other with a light color paint. The dark will make mending light color socks easier and vice versa.

• To hem a dress or skirt easily, use a plunger. Mark the handle at the desired length. As you pin or mark the hem, move the plunger around to make sure your line is straight.

• To make thread go through a needle more easily, spray the cut end with hair spray or starch.

• When sewing on heavy fabric, mark the lines with dry soap. The soap will make the needle go through without fuss or muss.

Pins and Needles

• Thread your safety pins onto a pipe cleaner and twist the ends together. As you need the pins, just untwist.

• You can punch extra holes in a belt if you heat a steel knitting needle.

• Hard-to-store needles, the extra long ones or the extra fine ones are best kept in an empty thermometer case.

• When you drop straight pins, you can pick them up quickly with a piece of cellophane tape or with a child's magnet.

• Stuck zippers can be opened by spraying them with starch...or by running a piece of dry soap along the teeth.

• Emblems so popular today can be stitched on in a jiffy. Dab the back of the emblem with water-soluble glue and press onto the garment. Then attach with thread either by hand or machine. The glue will dissolve in the next washing.

• Portable sewing machines are great but the foot pedal controls tend to creep. You can stop this annoying habit if you glue a thin piece of foam rubber to the bottom of your foot control.

• Blunt sewing machine needles are very handy for ripping out seams.

• To keep your sewing machine needles sharp, store them in a small bottle or tube to which a drop or two of oil has been added. Before using, wipe the needle with blotting paper.

• For quick oiling of a sewing machine needle, wipe it with a lock of your hair.

• Needles will not rust if you store them on a piece of waxed paper.

• Being prepared makes sewing a breeze. Pre-thread your needles. And remember, white and black are the most common colors used for mending and general sewing.

• When you oil your sewing machine, stitch through a piece of blotting paper several times before you sew on fabric. The blotting paper will absorb the excess oil.

Threads and Fabrics

• When using a single thread, it tends to knot. To stop this annoying problem, make the knot at the end that was cut from the spool. By doing this, the knot acts as a "weight".

• When the elastic sewed directly onto garments splits or becomes worn, just add a new piece of elastic to the damaged spot.

• To prevent knotting, run the thread through a cake of paraffin before you start to sew. The paraffin will not damage the fabric.

• When sewing a garment that is multi-colored—like tweed, for instance—use two or three strands of thread instead of one. Select the strands on the basis of the predominant colors of the garment. By doing this, the mended places will be less visible.

• When undoing a hem, you can save the thread to use again. Unwind the thread around the neck of a bottle. When you have all the thread on the neck, wet it and let it dry.

• Finding the right color thread is so much easier if you store the spools in plastic sandwich bags. All the reds in one bag, all the greens in another.

• Do you like to have your thread in view by your sewing machine? Place two nails in a line above your machine. String as many spools of thread as you wish on picture wire. Attach the ends of the wire to the nails. The more spools you want to string, the farther apart the nails should be.

• Empty thread spools are great for storing your tape measure.

• Slippery, sliding material like nylon and rayon will stay put if you cover the leaf of your machine with a pillow case.

Thread Care

• Drop mothballs into your balls of wool to keep them safe from you know what.

• Plastic rollers are handy for skeins of embroidery thread. Just unwind the thread onto the rollers.

• You can clean a skein of soiled white yarn this way: Sprinkle corn starch on the wool and wrap in a terry cloth towel. Wait forty-eight hours and shake out the starch.

• When mending knitted-type garments, use a vegetable brush to hold the cloth. The bristles cling to the cloth and make the damaged portion easier to sew.

Pattern Patter

• All commercial patterns require a 5/8" seam allowance. Lay a piece of colored tape 5/8" away from your sewing machine needle. Presto! An instant, visible, permanent guide.

• Protect the darts of your commercial patterns with cellophane tape. The darts will stay in longer and they will be easier to mark.

• When you have to adjust patterns by making extra pieces for them, use graph paper for a more accurate line.

• You can cut patterns without pins if you wish. Lay the paper pattern over the fabric and press with a hotish iron. The heat will cause the paper to cling.

• Paper patterns last longer when they are sprayed with fabric protector before they are used.

Knitting Notions

• You can ball your own yarn. Drop the skein over a revolving lampshade and roll into a ball.

• When you are done with your day's knitting, put a small cork on each needle. The stitches will stay put.

• The best way to store knitting needles? Line a box with corrugated paper and slip the needles into the grooves.

Do-It-Yourself Pincushions

• Cover a piece of steel wool and use it as a pincushion. Your needles will stay sharper.

• If you push a wad of cotton through the spool holes of your thread, it will make a handy pin cushion.

• A dry bar of soap makes a good pincushion. And your pins and needles will go through fabric with less push on your part.

Odds and Ends

• Many sewing projects call for using yarns of different colors. When you have a project like this, thread the yarns through one of those mesh bags that onions come in. Not only will this keep the yarns from getting tangled all together, but it will keep them from slipping onto the floor and getting dirty.

• When you have to sew some form of plastic, place a sheet of waxed paper between your needle and the object. You'll be amazed at how quickly the job gets done and with no puckering to speak of. This waxed paper trick also works very well on nylon and other sheer, difficult to sew fabrics.

- Store your remnants in plastic bags. Not only can you see what you have, but the fabric stays clean.
- When you are going to finish off something with a crocheted edge, run the item through your sewing machine. Use a large needle. The needle will make holes that are big enough to get a small crochet hook through.
- Letting down the hems of a little girl's dress may save money, but it often leaves a tell-tale mark. Sew a strip of rick rack along the hem mark. This hides the mark and gives the dress an attractive, new appearance.
- You can make your own standing yardstick by putting the end into a piece of modeling clay.
- When you want to clean your sewing machine around the bobbin, use the crevice attachment of your vacuum cleaner.
- For instant measuring, glue a tape measure along the edge of your sewing machine and secure it with a coat of varnish.
- You can turn your old full slips into half slips by cutting off and discarding the top half. Sew elastic around the waist of the bottom half.
- To mend large holes in clothing or sheets, place a piece of paper under the damaged area and stitch back and forth on your sewing machine. The paper will dissolve in the next washing.
- Iron on tape is ideal for lining home-made belts.
- Beads and sequins will be easier to sew on if you dip the needle in water first. The water will evaporate before you pull the needle through the fabric—therefore, no damage from the water.
- Ravel-prone fabrics will not unravel if you mark your sewing edge with crayon and stitch along this line.
- When making dresses for growing girls, leave some excess material at the waistline. As the girl grows, let the garment down from the waist rather than the hem.
- You can keep rick-rack, lace, and such like trimmings in place while you are sewing if you anchor them in place with a piece of cellophane tape.
- To give your sewing machine a clean sweep after each use, keep a soft pastry brush handy. Just sweep away the lint.
- Hate the feel of wool against your skin? Old nylon stockings make sweater liners, especially for the sleeves.
- Before cutting sheer, thin fabrics, give them a coat of spray starch. This reduces unraveling and gives the fabric more body so that it is easier to work with.

CHAPTER 5

HOUSE CLEANING FURNITURE

Leather

• For a protective shine on your leather upholstery, wipe off the surface dirt with a damp cloth. Then rub the leather with a cloth that has been dipped in well-beaten egg white. When the egg white dries, give the leather a final polishing with a soft, clean cloth.

• Leather upholstery also responds well to saddle soap applied with a damp cloth.

• To prevent your leather upholstery from cracking, polish it regularly with a cream made of one part white vinegar and two parts linseed oil.

• Leather chair seats can be cleaned by rubbing half a lemon over each and then polishing with a soft, clean cloth.

• Milk is a good preservative for leather. Wipe with a cloth that has been dipped in milk and the leather will keep its natural oils.

• When you find mildew on your leather upholstery, wipe it off with a cloth moistened with denatured alcohol.

• You can also clean your leather furniture with a cloth that has been dipped in a mild solution of chlorine bleach and water.

• Leather-topped tables are lovely and need care if they are to stay that way. Every few months remove the built-up wax with a solution of one quarter cup white vinegar and one half cup of water. The indentations caused by pressure from lamps and such can be removed by applying lemon to the leather twice a day for a week. If you use lemon oil once a month, it will prevent further marks from forming.

Vinyl

• Plastic and vinyl look quite well after they have been wiped with a solution of one tablespoon of washing soda added to one quart of water . . . baking soda or white vinegar sprinkled on a damp, slightly rough cloth also works well. Follow this method with a mild dish washing soap wipe. Oiling vinyl makes it hard. Vinyl is also hardened by body oils.

Slipcovers

• When you remove cotton slipcovers for a washing, put them back on while still ever so slightly damp. This saves ironing. And if you give the ruffles and pleats a good tug, you won't have to iron.

them either.

Wicker and Wrought Iron

• Wicker furniture, so popular again, needs moisture. In the winter, place a moisturizer near the furniture made of wicker.

• Wicker will not turn yellow if you wash it frequently with a warm water salt solution.

• In the winter, store your wicker garden furniture indoors. Freezing causes it to crack.

• Applying an occasional coat of lemon oil keeps wicker furniture from drying out.

• When your wrought iron furniture shows signs of rust, use turpentine to scrub the spots away.

Upholstery

• An artgum eraser is great for removing slight smudges and spots from cotton upholstery.

• Shaving soap, the spray can variety, removes most upholstery stains and smudge marks quite easily and quickly.

• Here's how to make your own upholstery cleaner: Add one cup of mild detergent to two cups of boiling water. Let the mixture cool until it forms a jelly-like substance and then whip it to a foam with a hand-mixer.

Table Tops

• For gleaming formica table tops, polish with club soda.

• Plastic table tops sparkle if polished with turtle wax...and toothpaste, followed by a good rub, works well, too.

• Small scratches on glass-topped tables can be removed with toothpaste. And for really gleaming glass tops, try this: Sprinkle the glass with lemon juice. Spread the juice with a paper towel and polish the top with a piece of newspaper.

Legs and Seats

• Table leg wobbly? Build up the leg this way: Place a small amount of plastic wood on a piece of waxed paper. Press the short leg into this and let it dry. Trim off any excess with a sharp knife and remove the rough edges with sand paper.

• When your cane chair seats begin to sag, pour boiling water over them and allow them to dry outside in the sunlight. This will make the cane shrink and tighten.

• When chair springs sag, turn the chair upside down and, using a piece of paper, make a pattern of the bottom. Trace the pattern on

63

a piece of plywood and cut out. Nail the wood to the bottom. This will force the springs back up into the chair. As a result, no more sag.

Furniture Polish

• Do you want to make your own furniture polish? Buy some BOILED linseed oil at your favorite hardware store. Mix together one third cup each of the boiled linseed oil, turpentine and white vinegar. Stir and shake well. Apply the polish with a soft cloth and wipe the wood completely dry with another. Polish with a third cloth. Or if you just want to boost the polishing power of your present product, add a teaspoon of cider vinegar and shake well.

• Here's another furniture polish you can make yourself—three parts olive oil and one part white vinegar. For a very high shine on wood furniture, rub in a solution of equal parts of lemon oil and turpentine. Wipe off the excess with a clean cloth. Buff the furniture with a soft wool cloth.

• Wrap your furniture polishing cloth in an old nylon stocking. The nylon serves to bring out just that much more sparkle!

• Liquid furniture polish can be messy. It drips, leaves marks during storage. To prevent this, when you are done with the polish, slip the bottle into an old sock. The sock will absorb the drips and drops.

• Before using your liquid furniture polish, warm it in a pan of hot water. The warmed polish will penetrate the wood more deeply.

Cleaning and Polishing Tips

• Wood furniture will resist water marks if a coat of paste wax is applied at least twice a year.

• The best polish for walnut furniture is BOILED linseed oil.

• Wipe varnished furniture with a cloth dipped in cool tea...or wipe with a cloth that has been dipped in a solution of one cup of white vinegar and one gallon of warm water.

• If your furniture has been oiled, don't try to wax it. Wax cannot be applied over oil.

• For intricately carved furniture, apply the wax or polish with an old toothbrush. To buff, wrap a piece of thin polishing cloth around another toothbrush.

• To bring out the luster of unpainted furniture, spread a dab or two of petroleum jelly on a damp sponge and apply to the furniture.

• When cleaning wrought iron furniture, use a cloth moistened with sweet oil. Rub the oil in thoroughly and polish with a woolen cloth. To keep the furniture clean, coat the furniture with a liquid wax. Fill in nicks and scratches with black crayon.

- Bottle brushes come in handy when cleaning metal furniture with hard-to-reach crevices.
- For maple furniture, mix a solution of equal parts of iodine and denatured alcohol. Apply the solution with a cotton swab. When it is dry, wax as usual and buff to a high shine.
- To remove furniture polish build-up, use a solution of one half cup of white vinegar and one half cup of water. Dip a clean soft cloth into the solution and wring it out. Wipe the furniture with the cloth and dry immediately with another cloth—a dry one.

Stains and Scratches

- Any scratches on teakwood should be rubbed very gently with steel wool first. Then rub in a solution of equal amounts of linseed oil and turpentine.
- Scratches on walnut furniture disappear when rubbed with a piece of walnut meat. Use the fresh, unsalted kind. Break the nut in half and rub the scratch with the broken half.
- Most cement-type glues can be removed from wood furniture if you rub the mark with cold, salad oil, or even peanut butter.
- When you find candle wax on your wood furniture, soften the wax with a hair dryer. Wipe up the melted wax with a paper towel and wash the stained area with a solution of white vinegar and warm water. Blot dry.
- If the scratch is small, cover it with a generous amount of white petroleum jelly. Leave the jelly on for at least twenty-four hours. Rub the jelly into the wood and wipe the excess away with a clean cloth. Wax or polish as usual.
- For larger scratches, cover with a crayon or wax stick of appropriate color.
- Scratches on light finished furniture can be covered with tan shoe polish. This method works only on glossy finishes.
- For ebony furniture, use black shoe polish, eyebrow pencil or crayon to cover the marks.
- For mahogany, cover the scratch with dark brown crayon. For red mahogany, use ordinary iodine and apply with a water color brush which can be purchased at an art supply store.
- For white marks made by liquids, put toothpaste on a damp cloth and rub into the stain. Sometimes adding a bit of baking soda helps...or you can make a paste of margarine or mayonnaise and cigarette ashes. Rub into the spot and buff with a slightly damp cloth. Finally, wax or polish as usual...or you can apply a paste of salad oil and salt. Let the paste stand for about five minutes and wipe away. Wax or polish as usual.

Cigarette Burns

• Here are some tips on covering cigarette burn marks...but if you are dealing with a very valuable piece of furniture, let a professional do the covering. These tips are meant for not-so-valued pieces. Most minor burns can be covered with mayonnaise. Rub in well and leave for fifteen or twenty minutes. Wipe off the mayonnaise with a soft cloth...you can also make a paste of rottenstone (which you can buy at a hardware store) and salad oil. Rub the paste into the burned area only using your fingertip and following the grain of the wood. Wipe the paste off with a cloth that has been dipped in oil and wipe dry with another cloth. Finish the job with a coat of your favorite furniture polish...or you can buy a wax stick at a paint or hardware store. These sticks come in a variety of colors. Scrape away the charred portion gently using a sharp knife. Take a heated knife blade and hold it against the stick until the wax melts. Smooth the melted wax over the damaged area with your finger. Let the wax harden before you polish or wax.

CHAPTER 6

POLISHING: METALS AND MARBLES

The gleam and shine of metal and marble is half the fun of owning these objects. Keeping them sparkling need not be either difficult or expensive.

Aluminum
• To remove stains on the outside of the object, rub with half a lemon. Wash and dry as you would normally.
• To remove stains on the inside of the object, fill with a quart of water. Add two tablespoons of vinegar or cream of tartar and boil ten to fifteen minutes. Wash and dry as you would normally.

Brass
• Mix equal parts of salt and ordinary white flour. Add just enough vinegar to make a thick paste. Rub it on the object liberally. Let the paste dry. Rinse it off with warm water. Dry with a clean, soft cloth. Or. . .
• Drop the brass pieces into a solution of equal parts vinegar and water. Soak for at least an hour. Scrub with a brush briskly. Rinse in warm water. Dry with a clean, soft cloth.

Bronze
• Go over with a soft cloth moistened with paraffin oil. Polish to a high shine with a clean chamois.

Chrome
• Use a solution of two cups of kerosene and one cup of rubbing alcohol. Apply with a damp cloth. Wipe dry. Or. . .
• Apply a thin coat of paste wax. The water will bead and roll off keeping the chrome bright and shiny. Or. . .
• Apply a small amount of peanut butter. Rub briskly and wipe off the excess. Or. . .
• Rub the chrome with ordinary white flour.

Copper
• If your copper pieces are not lacquered, coat them with clear cellulose lacquer which is available in hardware stores. The coating dries in about ten minutes and hardens in about an hour. Copper

cooking utensils cannot be lacquered. For those items:
• Fill a spray bottle with warm vinegar and add three tablespoons of salt. Spray the solution liberally on the copper. Leave the solution on for about ten minutes. Then rub the bottom clean with a cloth. Or...
• Dip lemon halves in salt and rub the copper. Rinse and dry. Or...
• You can make your own copper polish by mixing together
  ½ cup white vinegar
  ¼ cup table salt
  ¼ cup commercial cleanser
• If the copper is very dirty or tarnished, apply the above mixture with a soapless steel wool pad. If the copper is not too dirty or tarnished, apply the mixture with a damp sponge. Rinse with hot water and dry with a clean, soft cloth.

Marble
• Slice a lemon in half. Dip it in salt (plain borax can be used in place of salt, but plain old table salt is cheaper). Rub over the entire surface. Give the stains an extra hard rub. Allow to stand for five to ten minutes. Wash the surface with mild soap and water. Dry with a soft cloth.
• To maintain the clean white look, apply a thin coat of clear paste wax. Allow the wax to dry for five minutes. Wipe off and buff to a high shine with a soft, clean cloth.

Pewter
• Rub with cabbage leaves. Or...
• If you have a fireplace, save the WOOD ash. Take a tablespoon of ash and add enough water to make a paste and rub on with a damp sponge. Rinse and dry with a clean, soft cloth. Or...
• For heavily tarnished pewter, take a vitreous enamel pail. Add two gallons of warm water. Put the pewter piece in this solution and boil for two hours. Allow the solution to cool and remove the piece. Go over it with a commercial cleanser and give it a final polish with a brass polish. NOTE: When using the caustic soda solution, wear rubber gloves and make sure there is enough ventilation by your stove.

Silver
Silver flatware, whether sterling or plate, is becoming less of a luxury and more of an investment with each passing day. As the

price of gold continues to climb, so does the price of silver. And, so like any investment, your silver deserves maximum tender loving care with a minimum amount of effort on your part.

There is, however, some confusion about silver terminology. The following definitions will help you know what is what.

> **Sterling:** By law, to be considered sterling, a piece must be composed of a minimum of 92.5% pure silver and a maximum of 7.5% "base" metal which is usually copper.
>
> **Silver Plate:** This is any base metal, again usually copper, coated with pure silver. The thickness of the coating varies, but the more expensive plated pieces are heavily coated and therefore wear longer.
>
> **Electroplate:** This is silverplate, only the bond between the silver and the base metal is formed by a small current of electricity rather than by dipping the base piece into liquid silver. The bond is firmer and pieces can be plated more quickly.
>
> **Sheffield Plate:** This is silverplate made in the English city of Sheffield.

Silver, whether sterling or plate, is meant to be used. Keeping it tucked away for special occasions does it no good. This is particularly true for sterling which should acquire what is called a "patina". That's the warm, mellow shine that sterling acquires from use. The patina not only adds to the beauty of the silver, but also to the value.

Cleaning and Polishing Sterling and Plate

• For quick touch-ups, take a new powder puff (do not use the fleecy, woolly kind). Cut a small hole in the seam and spoon in a commercial cream polish. Keep the puff by your sink. As you are washing your silver, give the puff a quick dip in the water and go over any pieces that need a touch-up.

For a good cleaning, there are several methods. All are simple, easy, and inexpensive.

• Crush a sheet of aluminum foil and place it at the bottom of a glass baking dish. Arrange the pieces on it so that they do not touch each other. Fill the baking dish with boiling water and sprinkle two tablespoons of baking soda for each quart of water used. Let the pieces soak for at least five minutes, but no longer than ten. Or...

• Take an aluminum pan. Add one quart of water, a tablespoon of baking soda, and one tablespoon of salt. Bring this mixture to a boil in the pan. Drop your silverware into the boiling water a few pieces at a time. Let them boil for three to five minutes. Remove the pieces from the pan. Let them dry on a terrycloth towel. Buff to a high shine with another terrycloth towel. Or...

• Mix one tablespoon of ammonia, one tablespoon of powdered whitener (available in hardware stores), and two cups of boiling water. Let the mixture steep for fifteen minutes. The mixture will fizzle and foam, but don't worry about this. It's supposed to do this. Soak a terrycloth towel in the mixture and let the towel drip dry. Instead of drying your silver with an ordinary towel, use this treated one.

• Silver experts claim that intricately-patterned silver pieces should not be cleaned too thoroughly around the design. The blackening that builds up in the crevices of the pattern makes the design stand out more clearly. Some people, however, find the blackening unattractive. If you are one of them, get a commercial polish and apply to the design with a baby's toothbrush. This really cleans away the tarnish in those hard-to-reach places.

Stainless Steel

• Fill a dishpan with hot water. Add two tablespoons of bleach and soak the piece for several hours. Overnight, if possible. Wash in hot, soapy water. Or...

• When you are done with your dishes, squeeze out the dishcloth or sponge thoroughly. Rub it over a bar of soap. Then apply to your stainless steel pieces. Give a final polish with a dry cloth. This polishing trick is especially good for counter tops, stove hoods, tiles, etc.

CHAPTER 7

CHINA AND CRYSTAL

China and crystal, however lovely, are fragile. Therefore they need particular care. Whenever possible, store these items in a cabinet that you can reach without stooping or climbing. Having to go through such contortions makes chipping or breaking a piece more likely.

Storing

• For chinaware, use plastic storage bags that you find in the supermarket. These bags not only come in a variety of sizes, but they also last forever.

• For crystal, the best and safest way is to wrap the glass in tissue paper and keep them in cartons with the cardboard dividers. These cartons can be had FREE at any supermarket.

• When moving, wrap your china and crystal in sheets, towels, washclothes, etc. This means you will not have to wash the pieces during unpacking, and your hands stay clean.

Cleaning

• For gleaming crystal, wash in a solution of one cup white vinegar and three cups of warm water. No soap! Dry with a lint-free towel. The vinegar not only makes the crystal gleam, but it also keeps a good many germs under control.

• For crystal with intricately cut designs, scrub with a soft toothbrush—using the above solution. MONEY-SAVING TIP: Use a toothbrush that is ready for the scrap heap.

• To clean decanters and narrow-necked vases, use a mixture of sand and white vinegar. Let the mixture sit in the glass piece for half an hour. Swirl in one direction, then the other, and finally, shake up and down. Continue this every half hour (but not more than four hours) until the stain disappears.

• To restore the original high luster of chinaware, dip a sponge in lemon juice and sprinkle with salt. Rub until the desired level of luster has been reached. Rinse with hot water. Dry with a clean, lint-free cloth.

• To remove tea stains, sprinkle darkened area with baking soda or borax and rub with a damp sponge. Or . . .

• Soak the piece overnight in a solution of two quarts of water and half a cup of bleach. Wash thoroughly in hot soapy water. Or. . .

• Soak the piece overnight in a denture cleaner.

Repairs

• For small nicks and chips on crystal, rub the damaged area smooth with the fine side of an emery board. Polish with jeweler's rouge which is available in hardware stores and in jewelry shops.

• China can be repaired quickly with clear nail polish. After the polish dries, the excess can be wiped away with a cotton swab dipped in remover.

• To hold broken china pieces together while the mending agent is drying, use cellophane tape.

CHAPTER 8

CLEVER CLEANING CLUES

General Time Savers

• For busy housewives, a good cleaning schedule is to give one room a thorough cleaning once a week and just straighten the others. For example, Monday clean the kitchen, Tuesday, the living room, etc.

• A child's wagon can really help with the housework. As you start your cleaning chores, place all the equipment you will need . . . cloths, mops, disinfectants, steelwool pads . . . on the wagon and pull it around with you. This saves having to go back to your central storage closet each time you need something.

• The next time you defrost your refrigerator, spray the freezer compartment with non-stick cooking spray. When you have to defrost again, the ice will drop off more easily.

• Coating the areas around doorknobs and light switches with spray starch makes wiping off fingerprints and smudges easy.

• To make sure your candles do not drip and burn evenly, store them in your refrigerator for twenty-four hours before using them.

• Vinegar will cut grease on stovetops, refrigerators, walls painted with enamel or gloss.

Cleaning Pictures

• Pictures, even when protected by glass, can be dingy looking. To restore them, remove (and clean) the glass. Gently rub the picture with a piece of white bread. The bread will absorb the dirt and dust and, at the same time, leave a protective coat.

• Gilt picture frames can be wiped clean with beer. The beer does not harm gilt.

• Those long-handled brushes used to sweep snow off car windows have a great indoor use as well. The long handle allows you to clean the tops of pictures and high pieces of furniture without climbing and straining to reach.

Hard-to-Clean Spots

• Use the radiator attachment of your vacuum to clean the tops of books.

• An easy and safe way to clean grandfather and enclosed wall clocks...saturate a cotton ball with kerosene and leave it on the bottom of the clock case for several days. The kerosene fumes will loosen the dirt which will drop to the bottom of the case. All you have to do is wipe the accumulation up very gently.

• A cotton swab dipped in cleaning solution is handy for cleaning behind stove knobs and under the dial of your telephone.

Helpful Hints

• Here's a cleaning tip that protects your family's health: Once a day wipe the mouth and ear pieces of all your telephones with straight disinfectant. You'd be surprised what can be picked up from a telephone and the disinfectant cuts down the chances.

• Missing the knobs from a drawer and can't open it? Use a plunger. The suction will allow the drawer to pull open.

• To keep drawers from sticking, rub wax or dry soap along the sides and runners. If the drawer remains stubborn, lightly sand the areas where the sticking occurs.

• Leather desk sets should be treated with saddle soap to retain their fine appearance.

• Children's toy mops and brooms are handy items to clean those hard-to-reach places in your home.

• Cut a whisk broom at an angle to use for brushing out hard-to-reach corners and such.

• Wiping your wood furniture with a thin coat of cedar oil gives the room a delightful, long-lasting fragrance.

Bathroom Tips

• To avoid breakage and save time when cleaning a medicine cabinet, place a tray over the sink and use it as a temporary shelf.

• A thin coat of clean nail polish preserves labels on medicine bottles.

• To clean heavy shower stall build-up, rub lightly with a piece of dry, fine steel wool (not soap-filled). Be sure to test a small section first to be certain it won't scratch the tile.

• Glass shower doors will shine when rubbed with a sponge dampened in white vinegar.

• If you bath the family cat in the bathtub, drape an old bath towel over the side of the tub to let kitty dig her claws into. Gives her a more secure feeling. Likewise, dogs feel more secure if you place a rubber mat in the tub before bathing. Also, by stuffing a nylon scouring net into the drain hole, you will keep the pipe from becoming clogged with dog hair.

CHAPTER 9

FLOORS

Tool Care

• If you have a carpet sweeper, dampen the brushes with water before using. This trick will double the efficiency of your appliance.

• When you want to remove wax build-up from the pads of your floor polisher, wrap in several thicknesses of paper toweling. Press a hot iron on both sides of the toweling. The heat from the iron will melt the wax; the paper toweling will absorb it.

• To keep your mop, as well as your floor clean, cover your mop with an old nylon stocking. When you're done, just rinse the stocking out and let it dry for the next use.

• A dry mop is more efficient than a broom, especially in the kitchen. Crumbs and dust and such clings to a mop.

Floor Protection

• You won't mar your beautiful wood floors when moving furniture if you slip socks over the legs.

• Or when you have to move heavy furniture across wooden floors, slip the legs into empty milk or cream containers. Not only will this protect your floors, but the wax coating will make the whole process that much easier.

• And to keep your rocking chair from marking your floor, cover the rockers with adhesive tape. . .or coat the rockers with past wax.

Squeaky Floors

• Squeaky floor boards can be quieted forever if you sprinkle talcum powder between the boards. . .or dribble a wee amount of liquid glue between them.

• More hints for squeaky floor boards: Powdered graphite kills the squeak. Another trick, heat liquid soap in a sauce pan and squirt it between the boards.

Cleaning Wood Floors

• Wiping wood floors with plain water does more harm than good. Add turpentine or white vinegar to the water before wiping up the floors.

• When you find a coffee stain on your wood floor, rub it with a soapless steel wool pad that has been dipped in rubbing alcohol.

• Dampen your dry mop with a mixture of three parts kerosene and one part paraffin oil. The result is a nice shiny, clean floor.

• Moving furniture around without preventive care means ugly, dark marks on your wooden floors. To remove them, use a soapy cloth that has been sprinkled with kerosene.

• Scratches on wooden floors can be almost made to disappear if you rub them with a piece of soapless steel wool that has been dipped in paste floor wax.

• Faced with a faded floor? There's no need to refinish the whole floor. Combine brown shoe polish, the paste kind, with paste floor wax. Rub the worn, faded, spots and buff if necessary. The result is a warm, attractive antiqued look.

• Cold tea is a good cleaning agent for varnished floors (and woodwork, too). Just apply as you would any other liquid cleaner.

Caring for Linoleum and Tile Floors

• You can fix loose linoleum edges yourself. Buy some linoleum cement at your favorite hardware store. Then apply the compound with a dull knife. To hold the edge down until the cement dries, stack a few heavy books on the area.

• When your linoleum cracks, it's easy to fix, too. Cover the crack with a strip of cellophane tape. To keep the tape in place, cover with a coat of shellac.

• Heel marks can be removed from the floor with an ordinary pencil eraser . . . or, for more stubborn marks, moisten a cotton wad with kerosene or turpentine and rub until the marks disappear.

• Paste wax will remove tar spots.

• If you spill nail polish on waxed or tile floors, leave it until the polish is almost dry. Remove with a single-edge razor blade. For completely hardened polish, use nail polish remover. For smears, wipe them up before they dry. If the smear is dry, nail polish remover again.

• Silver polish will remove crayon marks from vinyl tile or linoleum floors.

• For a quick floor shine between waxings, wrap a piece of waxed paper around your dry mop and go over the floor. This trick also picks up loose dirt and dust. They adhere to the waxed paper.

Waxing and Cleaning

• When you do wax your floors, try to do it on a cold, dry day.

Warm, humid weather keeps wax from drying quickly.

• A very cheap and efficient floor polisher is an ordinary brick wrapped in two woolen socks.

• When you have to wipe spills and splashes from your linoleum floors, use milk instead of water. The milk protects the wax shine better than water.

• Instead of damp mopping your waxed floors every day, buff them lightly with a soapless steel wool pad. Water tends to cut into the wax and dull the shine.

• When applying paste wax by hand, use a glove-type pot holder. The fabric is quite strong and your hands and nails are completely protected from the wax.

• Hate to get down on your hands and knees to scrub away stubborn spots? You can avoid this. Place a steel wool pad under the sponge mop. Let the steel wool do the work as you guide it with your mop.

Cleaning Up Messes

• Ever try wiping up raw egg from your kitchen floor? Messy! Forget the cloth method. Cover the egg with salt and leave it for fifteen or twenty minutes. Then sweep it up!

• When you have to sweep up broken glass, ashes or dust, dampen two edges of a single sheet of newspaper and place it on the floor. Sweep the mess onto the paper. Using the dry edges, roll the paper up and toss it out.

• If you wrap your dry mop with paper towels, dusting waxed kitchen floors is easier. The dust clings to the towels.

• When you have to sweep up a pile of dust or ash, dampen the inside of your dust pan. The moisture will hold the fly-away stuff and cut down on sneezing.

• Alcohol spilled on asphalt tile causes white spots. Rub these spots with a little baby oil to remove them.

Carpets and Rugs

• Floor covering is meant to be walked on, and because of this, we constantly track dirt and sand from our shoes across the rugs. For this reason floor coverings should be cleaned everyday to avoid ground-in grime. But instead of hauling the vacuum on a daily basis, invest in an old-fashioned carpet sweeper. It's light, easy to use, and careful with energy.

• But you can do more with rugs than just walk on them. Slip an inexpensive braid rug under your stove, washer, dryer, any appliance that is too close to the floor to allow you to clean under it properly. The dirt and dust will adhere to the rug. From time-to-time, pull the rug out and wash it.

• Furniture leaves marks on the rugs. To remove them, pour water into the depression. Leave the water for at least eight hours. The nap will come up by itself. You can also lay a damp cloth over the marks and apply a moderately hot steam iron. Raise the nap by going over the marks with a stiff brush.

• All wool or wool blend rugs look their best when the natural oil content is maintained. Occasionally go over such rugs with a solution of one half cup of white vinegar and one quart of water. Apply with a sponge mop.

• Damp coffee grounds make a good sweeping compound. Sprinkle them over your rugs and work in with a damp sponge mop. Leave for half an hour and vacuum.

• Before you vacuum a rug cushion, cover it with a piece of window screen. This will let you remove the dirt without pulling the cushion to pieces.

Throw Rugs

• If your rug rolls up at the edges, place a heavy matting of newspaper under the corner. Dampen the curling corner. As the rug dries, it will flatten itself out.

• Tired of throw rugs that won't stay flat? Turn the rug over and apply two coats of clear shellac to the underside. Let the shellac dry between coats.

• When a shag rug becomes limp and laggard from too many washings, apply a strong liquid starch to the back. Let the starch dry thoroughly before you put the rug back on the floor.

• Want to get rid of the lint that accumulates on throw rugs? Pop them in your dryer for ten minutes. . .or, if you don't have a dryer, hang them outside for an hour or so, and the windier the day, the better.

• For really bright rugs and carpets, sprinkle them with a generous amount of salt. Leave the salt for at least an hour and then vacuum the rug.

• Never drag furniture across your carpets as this can, and often does, damage the fibers. Lift the furniture up and carry it away.

• Flat nap can be revived if you dampen the rug and brush the indented areas with a coin.

• A damp chamois cloth, folded several times and placed over a carpet depression will also raise the nap again.

• Curling carpet corners can be flattened if you place a damp cloth on the area and run a hot iron over the corner—both front and back.

• To make sure your carpets stay flat, sew a piece of cardboard cut in the shape of an L at each corner.

• Scatter rugs will stay put if you place a rubber bath mat under them...or you can attach rubber canning jar rings to each corner. Coating the underside with rubberized spray also helps.

• The thinnest rug can feel heavenly thick if you place a foam rubber pad under it.

• If your floors are uneven, level your rugs with carpet cushions. This will reduce the wear. To further reduce wear, rotate the position of your rugs once a year.

• Wool rugs last longer if there is some humidity in the air. Fiber rugs are helped by an occasional spraying with water. They should not, however, be soaked.

• While many old fashioned methods are coming back into style, stay away from rug beating. It can crack the backing of the rug.

• If you roll a rug diagonally, it will not buckle while it is being carried. And if you must store a rug up-ended, place a pole of some sort in the middle to provide support.

• Fringe can be attached to a rug without sewing. Use masking tape.

• For small apartments, use matching floor covering throughout. This will give the impression of more room.

Carpet Cleaning

• When you have your carpet removed for cleaning and you do the floors, wait at least two days before re-installing the rugs. By putting the carpet down sooner, you risk mildew.

• For a quick carpet cleaning, mix a solution of plain ammonia and warm water. Go over the carpet with a damp sponge mop.

• If you do your own rug shampooing, rub the nap up with a brush.

• You can dry clean your carpets. Sprinkle salt on the rug and vacuum. You get a bright clean rug and the salt helps to moth-proof wool rugs. You can also go over your rugs with a salt solution. Use a sponge mop. Another dry cleaning method is to brush a mixture of salt and cornmeal into your rugs. Wait an hour or so and vacuum.

• When using a carpet sweeper, dampen the brush first. Lint will be easier to pick up. For those ever-visible lint pieces and bits of thread, use a stiff toothbrush.

79

• If you use a diagonal stroke when vacuuming area rugs, they will be less likely to get caught up in the vacuum.

• Never rub stains on your rugs and carpets. Blot with paper towels. Rubbing only pushes them deeper into the pile.

Carpet Spot Removals

• You can remove crayon marks from rugs with cellophane tape. Rub the sticky side against the mark.

• For a cigarette burn on a light carpet, use liquid bleach, a mild solution, to take out the black mark. For dark carpets, pull some fuzz from an inconspicuous spot and roll into a ball the size of the burn mark. Put a drop or two of strong glue in the burn hole. Press the fuzz ball into the burn hole. Cover the repair job with a piece of tissue held down by a heavy object. The glue will dry slowly which is what you want for the best results.

• Shaving cream makes a good instant all around spot remover for rugs and carpets.

• Food coloring makes a good cover-up for bleach stains on your rugs and carpets. And artgum erasers will remove soot marks.

• For candle drippings, cover with a piece of blotting paper. Press down with a hot iron. Keep repeating the process until all the wax has been taken up.

• Braided rugs which come apart at the seams can be repaired with fabric glue. This method is fast and easy.

• If your rugs and carpets are spotted with old stains, try this method. Mix a solution of two tablespoons detergent, three tablespoons of vinegar and one quart of warm water. Work this solution into the stain and blot up as much moisture as you can with paper towels.

• Stains can be removed from outdoor carpeting with regular prewash spray. Apply a liberal amount to the carpet and leave it for fifteen minutes or so. Hose the carpet down.

• When you have a wet or damp carpet and don't want rust marks, wrap the legs of all metal-tipped furniture in little plastic sandwich bags.

• Damp mud will leave no marks if you sprinkle with salt. Leave the salt on the mud for about fifteen minutes and then vacuum. The salt absorbs the mud.

• Red wine stains on carpets can be removed with white wine.

• Glue will lift off carpets and rugs if you saturate the spot with white vinegar. As the glue softens, lift it off.

80

CHAPTER 10

WALLS, WINDOWS AND FIREPLACES

Wallpaper

• An unsightly bulge in your wallpaper? Slit it with a sharp razor blade. Using a toothpick, put some glue under the paper. Smooth the paper down with a damp sponge.

• Grease spots can be removed from wallpaper! Make a paste of cornstarch and water. Apply to the grease spot and leave until dry, then brush off. This method sometimes requires several applications ...you can also apply a piece of blotting paper to the grease spot and apply a warm iron. The heat melts the grease and the paper absorbs it. This method also may have to be repeated. Use a clean piece of blotting paper for each application. You can also make a paste of Fuller's Earth and carbon tetrachloride (you can buy both at most hardware stores) and apply it as you would the cornstarch paste. Remember, follow the directions for using carbon tetrachloride very carefully.

• As for crayon marks, treat them as a greasy spot. You can also rub the spot with baking soda sprinkled on a damp cloth. A light rub with a dry steel wool soap pad also works well.

• Ordinary fingerprints and dirt smudges can be removed from wallpaper with an artgum eraser which is sold in stationery stores.

• When you want to remove cellophane tape from wallpaper, press a warm iron against it. The tape will peel off.

• If you place a small rubber bumper along the bottom of your pictures and mirrors, the air will circulate, and you won't have your walls marked with black streaks.

• Cover your dry mop with a piece of flannel and wipe your wallpaper. The flannel removes the dust and brightens the paper.

Walls

• Walls and woodwork should always be washed from the bottom up to keep streaks from forming along the unwashed area. And the best solution for washing painted walls...mix one half cup ammonia, one quarter cup of white vinegar, one quarter cup of washing soda, and one gallon of warm water. Stir well.

• When washing your shellacked wood-paneled walls, sprinkle a few drops of white vinegar on a damp cloth and wipe. Go over the walls with a dry cloth immediately.

• When you have to remove crayon marks from painted walls, use lighter fluid...or rub briskly with a terry towel.

• Sooty walls can be vacuumed. Indeed, it is always best to vacuum your walls before washing to remove any surface dust.

• If your walls are paneled with brown-stained wood, clean them with a cloth moistened in a solution of one part warm water and one part lemon oil. Not only does this remove the dirt, but it also restores the gleam.

• A nylon or banlon sock is the best cleaning cloth for rough-plastered walls.

• Cobwebs are easy to remove this way...slip an old sock or two over a yardstick and secure with a rubber band. Saves stretching and climbing. But best of all, the cobwebs really cling to the socks.

Wood Paneling

• Greasy woodwork can be cleaned easily in a number of ways... Mix a solution of starch and warm water and apply to the woodwork with a sponge. When the solution has dried, rub it off with a soft, clean cloth...or dip a cloth in turpentine and go over the woodwork...or mix a quart of warm water, a tablespoon of washing soda, and a quarter teaspoon of detergent. Apply with a sponge or damp cloth...or a brush, if you like!

• Ordinary pencil and art gum erasers also remove marks from woodwork.

• When you want to repair scratched woodwork, even deep ridges, fill them with a mixture of fine sawdust and spar varnish (available at hardware stores). After the mixture has dried, go over the area with fine sandpaper and then paint.

• You can remove paper stuck to a wood surface this way: Apply a few drops of baby oil. Leave for several minutes and then rub off with a clean, soft rag.

• The best washing solution for enamel painted woodwork is a half cup of kerosene to a gallon of warm water. Do not, however, use a cellulose sponge to apply. It will dissolve. Use a cloth of some sort. And don't fret if the kerosene floats on top of the water; it's supposed to.

• Glossy paint on woodwork will stay that way if you wipe it down with a mixture of a mild soap and milk.

Plaster

• When your plaster walls and ceilings start to crack, here's how to avoid an immediate and expensive replastering job. Make a paste of Elmer's glue and baking soda. If you are repairing a colored area, add a few drops of food coloring. Apply the paste to the cracks with your fingers.

• To cover nail holes in plaster walls, fill them with white toothpaste and smooth down with a damp sponge.

• Before repairing really large cracks in your plaster walls and ceiling, stuff them with newspaper or soapless steel wool and then repair.

Window Washing

• Windows will stay cleaner longer if you vacuum your screens frequently.

• Avoid washing windows on a sunny day. The sun's heat causes the window to dry too quickly and streak. Cloudy, overcast days are best. Never use soap when washing windows. It is one of the major causes of streaking.

• Want to make your own window washing solutions? Mix together one half cup of ammonia, one half cup white vinegar and two tablespoons of cornstarch to a bucket of warm water. If you like the "blue" kind, fill a spray bottle with three tablespoons of ammonia, one tablespoon of white vinegar. Add cool water. For the color...a few drops of blue food coloring.

• For a fast wash for just a few windows, use a sponge that has been saturated in white vinegar.

• Cola-type sodas cut right through any grease on your windows.

• Windows should be polished with newspapers or the tissue used in gifts. Unlike paper or cloth towels, they leave no lint.

• If you wipe the inside of your windows vertically and the outside horizontally, you will know immediately on which side any smudges are.

• For a final high shine, go over your windows with a clean blackboard eraser. The felt makes the glass sparkle.

• Old nylon stockings also give a high, bright shine to windows.

• When you feel you need privacy from prying eyes, you don't have to replace a clear pane of glass. Dissolve one tablespoon of epsom salt in a small amount of beer. Brush this solution on the inside window pane. When dry, the solution has an attractive crystalline look. It can also be washed off easily.

Curtain Care

• You don't have to take down your curtains and drapes every time you wash windows. Loop the curtains and drapes through metal hangers and suspend from the rods.

• Old door keys and fishing sinkers are great items to use when you need something to weight down your drapery hems.

• Give your traverse rods a coat of paste wax to keep them moving freely.

• Push your drapery hooks through a bar of soap before you thread them through the fabric. With the soap coating, the hooks are easier to push through the material.

Window Protection

• You can keep birds from soiling your windows by sprinkling moth crystals on the outside. The odor will keep them far away.

• A cracked pane of window glass can be temporarily waterproofed if you apply a coat of clear shellac over the split.

• Windows that rattle can be silenced by attaching a felt corn pad to the lower inside edge of the window. You can also drive several rubber-headed tacks against the bottom edges of the lower sash. When you close the window, the tacks will take up the slack.

• When you want to remove a pane of glass, run a red-hot poker along the putty. When you replace the pane, mix paint with the putty, to match the window frames. This saves you the job repainting when the glass is replaced.

Winter Window Problems

• When washing windows in the winter, add one half cup of rubbing alcohol or anti-freeze to the water. This will keep the windows from freezing up as you clean away.

• To prevent frost build-up during the cold weather months, dip a sponge in rubbing alcohol, anti-freeze or glycerine and coat the inside of the glass. Polish with a piece of newspaper.

• And another winter window problem is accumulated moisture which drips all over the place. When this happens, take several facial tissues and wipe nearly all the moisture off. Wipe from the bottom up for more satisfactory results. Then put a drop or two of liquid detergent on a tissue and coat the window. Again, work from the bottom up. The glass will be fuzzy for a second or so but will soon clear. The next time moisture accumulates, the detergent coating will make wiping the moisture off easier.

• The best way to clean spotted window sills is with a bit of rubbing alcohol. Not only does this remove the dirt, but it also gives the paint a fresh look.

Shades and Blinds

• Small rips and tears in window shades can be fixed with a coating of colorless nail polish.

• If you cannot wash your window shades, rub them with a piece of coarse flannel that has been dipped in flour or corn meal.

• You can keep your parchment shades clean by giving them a coat of paste wax. For small spots and smudges, use an artgum eraser.

• To brighten the tapes of your venetian blinds, apply white liquid shoe polish with a damp sponge. To clean the slats quickly, saturate a soft cloth in rubbing alcohol, wring it out, and secure the cloth to a rubber spatula.

• To make sure that your tieback curtains are straight, set your window shade or venetian blind at the level you want for the tiebacks. Use that as your guide. It never fails.

Frames and Screens

• To prevent your windows from sticking, coat the inside molding with petroleum jelly at least once a year.

• To loosen a stuck window, give the divider a sharp rap to one side. For older style windows, give the window rope or chain a vigorous snap. That usually loosens the most stubborn window.

• Aluminum window frames can be cleaned with ordinary silver polish.

• The easiest way to clean sliding door and window tracks is with an eraser. Secure a small piece of cloth to the bottom of a pencil and rub away the dirt.

• If you don't want spiders and other creepy things moving into your aluminum door and window tracks, coat them liberally with a commercial insect spray.

• Coating aluminum door and window tracks with spray starch keep them gliding smoothly.

• To quick-clean screens, go over them with a brush-type hair roller. You will be amazed at the amount of dust and dirt that adheres to the roller. When you are done, rinse the roller.

• For a more thorough job of cleaning, go over the screens with your vacuum. Next wipe both sides of the screen with kerosene and wipe dry with a clean cloth.

• When you remove your triple tracks for cleaning, can't remember which goes where? The next time you remove the storms and screens, mark them for easy replacement with nail polish. Here's an easy code...I for inside, M for middle, and O for outside.

• Do you have the old-fashioned screens and storms? The ones that must be taken down and replaced with each change of season? Again, a simple code helps. Using nail polish, paint a number on the inside window sash. Put the same number on the corresponding storm and screen. When the time comes to switch, all you have to do is match up the numbers. Sure saves time!

Fireplaces

Fireplaces have always been popular. For some people, they are a nice, cozy addition to any room. For others, fireplaces are romantic. And today as the price of fuel oil goes up, a fireplace is becoming a pleasant way to reduce heating costs.

• For really quick clean-ups, place a piece of aluminum foil under the grate.

• Toss a handful of table salt over your burning logs from time-to-time. This will greatly reduce the soot.

• For a really lovely aroma, add orange peels to burning logs.

• Here's how to remove the smoky smell from your fireplace when the season is over: Wash the floor and sides with a solution of warm water and three tablespoons of baking soda. The soda acts to neutralize the odor. Baking soda in water is also good for cleaning grimy bricks.

• White vinegar is ideal for cleaning brick tile around fireplaces. Apply with a small scrub brush and sponge dry.

• Regular artgum erasers will remove smoky spots from porous rock. For smooth stone or brick fireplaces, remove as much soot as you can with the artgum eraser. Then wash with a solution of trisodium phosphate and warm water. Use a solution of one half cup of trisodium to each gallon of water . . .

• For a really good cleaning, try this: Add a quarter cup of naptha soap to one quart of hot water. Heat until the naptha dissolves and cook. Add eight ounces of powdered pumice and a half cup of clear ammonia. Stir thoroughly. Next remove as much soot as you can. Apply the cleaning solution with a paint brush. Leave it on for thirty minutes. Scrub the bricks with a brush dipped in warm water. Rinse thoroughly with a clean sponge dipped in clean water.

• The bright red brick color of your fireplace will come back if you apply mineral oil with a pastry brush. The mortar will look brand-new white if you apply white liquid shoe polish with a small brush.

• Before you pack away your fireplace tools for the summer months, coat them with clear shellac. This will prevent rust from forming while in storage.

CHAPTER 11

PAINT AND PAPERING POINTERS

The appearance of any room perks up after a coat of paint or after fresh wallpaper is hung. But the redecorating process can be sloppy! And wallpapering! It may stick to you but not the walls. These pointers are meant to help cut back on the mess...

Mixing Paint

• Paint should be stirred and not shaken. And the best stirrer around is an old wire coat hanger. Straighten the hook and bend the sides until they almost meet.

• To mix your paint—pour it from one container to another as this speeds the mixing process and assures that the pigment is completely blended with the oil.

• If you have a small can of paint, use a heavy-duty plastic picnic fork to stir.

• Paint dries slightly darker than the mix. You might want to lighten what you see in the can.

• An old nylon stocking is a good paint strainer. So is a piece of fine screening or fine nylon netting.

• If you want to make sure your white paint stays truly white, add a drop or two of black paint and stir well.

• When you find that the paint in the can has completely separated, drain off the liquid at the top. Mix what is in the can thoroughly and slowly add the liquid back. Stir well.

Applying Paint

• You can do away with having to scrape windows if you moisten strips of newspaper and stick them on the window panes...or rub a bar of soap on the window...or pour some liquid detergent into a can and brush it on your windows. When the detergent is dry, it's time to paint.

• Before you start to paint window frames, clean out the accumulated dirt from the corners with a good stiff brush.

• When you do get paint on your windows, you can scrape it off with a copper penny. The coin will not scratch the class.

• When scraping window glass, don't scrape the putty off completely. Leave about 1/16th of putty all around the window. That's what holds the pane in place.

• Before you paint a surface that has been covered with whitewash, wash the surface with a strong baking soda solution.

• To remove some of the glare from freshly painted enamel, wipe the surface with a clean cloth dipped in turpentine.

• Enamel paint goes on more easily and smoothly if you let the can sit in a pan of hot water before you start.

• When painting the ceiling, instead of climbing up and down a ladder, extend the handle of your roller. And, too, paint a ceiling by walking back and forth the width and not the length of the room.

• If you add two teaspoons of oil of citronella or oil of wintergreen to your paint (per gallon), the insects will stay away until the paint dries.

Painting Tools

• If you get a brush hair on a freshly painted surface, remove it with a pair of tweezers.

• A cotton swab dipped in paint is ideal for small paint jobs. There's no brush to clean afterwards as you throw the swab out.

• Baby food jars are good containers when you are using just a small amount of paint.

• Another good container for small amounts of paint is an empty half pint heavy cream carton. Leave the pourer on until after you have added the paint. It makes the final stir easier. Then cut the top off.

Stairs

• There's a trick to painting stairs—although it takes two days. On day Number One, paint every other step. The next day, paint the other ones. Or you can paint just half of each step on Day Number One and finish the job on the following day.

Paint Problem Prevention

• Before you start to paint, rub petroleum jelly on your door hinges. Any paint splatters can be wiped off quickly and easily. And you won't have to take the doors off their hinges.

• To prevent a can of paint from tipping over, cut a hole in a large, empty box of detergent. The hole should be big enough to hold the can of paint. Detergent and soap boxes are best for this because they are made of stronger cardboard than, say, cereal boxes.

• Radiator covers should be painted when they are warm, rather than when they are cold or hot. The medium temperature will bake on the paint. Flat wall paint or enamel are best for radiator covers. You get better heating efficiency.

• Before you start to paint any surface, make sure it is clean or else the paint will not adhere well.

Time Savers

• Sponge mops make good paint applicators when a brush or a roller are unavailable.

• Line your paint pan with a sheet of aluminum foil. It saves clean up time and keeps the pan ready for the next application.

• When you first open a new can of paint, punch a series of small holes around the rim. As you wipe off excess paint from the brush, it will dribble right back into the can instead of slopping over the side.

• A paint roller attached to a mop handle makes painting floors easier. A cellulose sponge works quite well.

• Protect your ceiling fixtures with plastic bags. And remove the light bulbs before you start or you might break them.

• Painting ceilings can be drippy. But not if you slip a large paper plate under the roller or a piece of rubber matting...even one half of a large rubber ball.

Drips and Splatters

• Cover your doorknobs with plastic sandwich bags or aluminum foil before you start to paint. They will be protected from dripping paint.

• Paint spatters on window glass can be removed with nail polish remover. Dab on the remover with a ball of cotton. Leave for a few minutes and wash off with warm soapy water. This usually works even for paint that has been on the window for a long time.

• Paint stains on glass can also be dissolved with turpentine. A solution of hot water and vinegar works well, too. If you want to avoid drips and splatters on your woodwork, coat it with a bit of lemon oil before you start to paint. Any drips and what have you, will wipe away when you are done.

• Glue a large paper plate to the bottom of your paint can. The plate will catch the brush drips and not your floor.

• To keep paint off your shoes, wear an old pair of socks. Just pull them on over your shoes.

• To prevent splatters when you are mixing paint, wrap the can in a sheet of newspaper that is higher than the can.

• It is important that the rim of the paint can stay clean if you plan to store the unused portion for any length of time. If you wrap the rim in aluminum foil and tuck beneath the inside portion, the rim will stay paint free.

How Much Paint?

• You can estimate the amount of paint you will need for a radiator if you measure the front area and multiply by seven.

• A good rule of thumb is that a gallon of paint will cover six hundred feet on the first coat and approximately nine hundred square feet on the second.

Storing Paint

• So you can remember how much paint is left in a can, paint a line outside the can at the appropriate level.

• Before replacing the lid, place a disc of aluminum foil or waxed paper over the paint. You can get the right size disc by placing the can on the covering and cutting around it. Lay the covering over the paint and press down gently to remove the air bubbles. Replace the lid tightly. When you next use the paint, stir well.

• Your oil base paint will stay fresh if you spread four tablespoons of mineral oil over the top. Do not stir until you use the paint again.

• After you have resealed the lid, store the unused paint upside down to prevent paint scum from forming.

• Before sealing a can of paint, pour a little into clean empty nail polish or rubber cement bottles. This will allow you to make quick touch-ups without pulling out the paint can or getting a brush dirty.

• Before replacing the lid, breathe over the paint to prevent scum from forming. A few drops of paint thinner sprinkled on the surface will help keep your paint fresh. To really keep paint fresh for a long period of time, add a thin layer of melted paraffin across the top before sealing the can.

• Before sealing a lid on a paint can, make your own color chart. Either dip a popsicle stick or a strip of white cardboard into the paint. When it is dry, attach it to the can with a rubber band. You can take the chart with you when you go to select accessories for the room.

Brushes – Cleaning and Storing

• Before you use a new paint brush, soak it in linseed oil for twelve hours. After the oil treatment, it will not only last longer, but it will also be easier to clean.

• A soak in hot vinegar followed by a wash in warm sudsy water will soften a hard brush.

• After you wash your paint brushes and rollers, add fabric softener to the final rinse water. This treatment will keep them soft and pliable.

• When you clean your brushes with paint thinner, use a coffee can with a plastic lid. After the brushes are clean, cover the can and leave for several days. The paint will sink to the bottom and you can pour off the thinner and reuse it.

• To keep brushes from curling during cleaning, use a coffee can with a plastic lid. Cut holes slightly smaller than the brushes in the plastic lid. Push the brushes through the lid, handles first. Add the paint cleaner to the coffee can and snap the lid on. Your brushes will clean without curling.

• After you have cleaned your brushes, wrap them in plastic bags. Tie the bags tightly. Masking tape is particularly good for this purpose.

• If you have to stop in the middle of a painting job, wrap the brushes in aluminum foil and put them in the freezer. Take them out an hour or so before you start painting again.

• When your paint brushes are stiff with dry paint, soak them for about two hours in a solution of two tablespoons of salt, one cup of kerosene, and one quart of warm water.

• After you have cleaned your paint brushes, apply a thin coat of petroleum jelly. This acts as a preservative.

• Should your paint brush start to shed its bristles, apply a thick coat of clear nail polish to the base of the brush. That will hold the bristles fast.

Painting Furniture

• To antique a piece of furniture, use a small piece of carpet to work in the glaze. The carpet gives a more grained effect.

• To remove all dirt and dust, go over unpainted furniture with a piece of sandpaper. Then go over the piece with a vacuum cleaner and paint.

• Turpentine and olive oil mixed in warm water will remove wax build-up from your furniture.

• You can do small touch-ups on your furniture this way. Mix oil paint to match the finished color. Apply the paint with a tooth pick.

• Unpainted furniture can be stained with regular fabric dye. This gives you a wider choice of colors.

• When painting a dresser, take the drawers out. Place them so

91

that the fronts face up. This positioning will keep the paint from dripping all over the place.

• Before painting a table or a chair, hammer a small, sturdy nail halfway into each. The nails will allow you to paint the legs all the way to the bottom without the piece of furniture sticking to the floor or newspaper. Another thing you can do is place fairly large jar lids under each leg to catch any drips.

• The undersides of chairs and tables should be painted first. This way, you can turn the piece upright to finish the job.

• Before painting a piece of furniture, remove the knobs and other hardware. To keep the screw holes free of paint, stuff them with matchsticks.

• To cover drawer knobs with paint—easily—insert the screws halfway into the holes. Dip the knobs into the paint and let the excess drip off. Rest the base of the screws in pieces of modeling clay until the paint is dry.

• When dealing with reed or wicker furniture, you will get a more professional looking job if you use spray paint.

Decorating Tips

• When you want to lighten a dark corner, apply a coat of luminous liquid plastic paint.

• Ceiling too high for comfort? Paint it a darker color than the walls and it will appear to be lower than it is.

• Want your painted doors to have a smooth, velvety look? Sand the surface between coats. Make sure, though, that each coat is completely dry before you start to sand.

• You can apply paint to door bottoms without removing the hinges if you use a soft toothbrush.

• If you want to make a small room seem bigger, use light colored paint. If you want to make a large room seem smaller, use dark colored paint.

• When you want your narrow hallways to seem wider than they are, paint one wall with a dark shade of your color and the other with a light shade. In other words, one side is dark blue and the other light blue.

Wallpaper

• Here's a quick rule of thumb to decide how much wallpaper you need: Multiply the distance around the room (in feet) by the height of the room and then divide by thirty. For each average-sized window or doorway, deduct two rolls of wallpaper. Your final answer equals the number of wallpaper rolls you will need. This formula allows for matching.

• When you are repapering, give the old paper a thin coat of shellac. This will keep the seam marks from the old paper from showing through the new.

• While you are wallpapering, place dampened newspapers along the baseboards. The damp paper will catch and settle most of the fine dust.

• To prevent peeling in rooms that tend to be steamy, like bathrooms, give all seams a coat of clear varnish after the wallpaper paste has dried.

• Remember, when hanging washable paper, use a moisture-resistant or waterproof glue.

• Once the wallpaper glue is completely dry, go over the paper with clear shellac. This will keep the colors from fading and will be easier to clean.

• When using fabric as a wallcovering, you can remove all the wrinkles by spraying with water.

• When your wallpapering job is finished, wrap any leftover paper in aluminum foil and store in a dry place. The foil will keep the paper clean and bright and should you ever need a patch, it's readily available.

• Keep track of your wallpapering statistics. Write the number of rolls you used on the back of a picture that will hang in the room. The next time you want to repaper, all the information is hanging before you.

• Want to remove old wallpaper? You can run a paint roller soaked in hot water over the paper...for stubborn pieces, apply a steam iron...or saturate the paper with a solution of hot water and powdered laundry starch...or spray with a solution of two tablespoons of vinegar to a pint of water. Once the paper is loose, remove with a wide-blade scraping tool.

Plaster and Varnish

• When you are doing a small plastering job, keep the mixture in one half of a rubber ball. When you are done, flip the ball inside out and the remaining plaster will be released.

• Substitute evaporated milk for water if you want a stickier plaster of Paris mixture.

• A quick plaster for small jobs...mix equal parts of starch and salt. Add just enough water to form an adhesive.

• To save yourself the trouble of sandpapering after you apply plaster, wipe off the excess with a stiff paint brush.

• To keep your plaster soft and workable, add a few drops of white vinegar. This retards the hardening process.

• You will find varnish easier to work with if you keep the can in a pot of hot water. This makes the varnish dry faster, too.

• For a really natural finish, use orange shellac on dark woods and white shellac on light woods.

• Here's how to remove old varnish: Add three tablespoons of baking soda to one quart of water. Apply this solution with a rough cloth...or you can apply this mixture with a stiff bristled brush. Wipe the old varnish off with a rag. There should be no gumminess or odor.

• There are a number of ways you can remove paint stains from your hands...lighter fluid...cooking or baby oil...peroxide...a handful of sawdust mixed with turpentine...petroleum jelly. No matter which method you use, wash your hands thoroughly with soap and water. Dry well and apply some moisturizing hand cream. Of course the best thing to do is to make sure you do not get paint stains on your hands. Before you start to paint, rub a thin coat of petroleum jelly into your hands.

• To remove paint stains from clothing, scrape off any loose particles, hold the stained area over a boiling pot of water, and rub well with soap. A solution of equal parts of turpentine and household ammonia also dissolves paint stairs on clothing.

• For tiny splatters of paint, remove them with nail polish remover.

• You can make your own paint remover—mix together two parts of household ammonia and one part tupentine. Apply this mixture with a stiff brush. Leave it on for a few minutes and then remove with a clean, dry cloth.

• Never leave a can of turpentine uncovered. Water will condense on it causing the liquid to become cloudy and less effective.

• Wax of any kind causes paint to peel. For this reason, baseboards and window sills should not be waxed.

• An old baby bottle is perfect for mixing stains—or anything else that must be measured carefully. The ounce markings let you know where you are.

• You can strain sediment out of paint solvent or other thin liquids this way: Stuff a piece of soapless steel wool into the opening. Pour this liquid from the old container into a new one.

• Before painting a room, remove all the outlet plates. Paint them separately or else they will stick to the wall.

CHAPTER 12

ENERGY: HOW TO CONSERVE IT
WHILE CUTTING ITS COST

"Conserve Energy and Cut Energy Costs" may well become the motto of the nineteen-eighties. As monthly fuel and utility bills go higher and higher, the "cut to conserve" philosophy becomes more attractive. The following are ways to cut back on your energy consumption without having to resort to kerosene lamps:

Light

• Instead of several low watt bulbs in a room, use one large one. One 100-watt bulb gives fifty percent more light than four 25-watt bulbs, yet it uses the same amount of electricity.

• Whenever you dust a room, don't forget the lightbulbs and lampshades. You can increase the amount of light you get from a single lamp as much as fifty percent! Lampshades should be dusted inside and out.

• Colored light bulbs may be a glamorous decorating touch, but they waste electricity. The plain ones give more light.

• Cover your lamps with light transparent shades for maximum efficiency. Dark shades reduce the amount of light you receive.

• Whenever you leave a room for more than five minutes, turn out the lights. Less than five minutes, it really does not pay to turn the lights off since a constant flipping of the switch up and down is also wasteful.

• Thinking of repainting your home? Give thought to light colors. You'll need less lamp light to see in the room.

Refrigerator

• Your refrigerator should be far away from your stove, or any other source of heat. When a refrigerator is too close to a heat source, the motor works harder to maintain a cool tememperature.

• Before refrigerating, let foods cool to room temperature. Placing hot foods in the fridge means using more electricity than necessary to cool them off.

• Going away for vacation or even a long weekend? Empty your refrigerator and turn it off. If this is not practical, lower the temperature control. Unplug electric clocks. Turn off the water heater. If you have a gas stove, seal off the pilot lights. And don't forget to lower your automatic thermostat. Unplug TV sets.

• When you plan to be out of your house for several hours, raise the thermostat in the winter and the air conditioner in the summer.

• Check the gasket on your refrigerator door several times a year. Close the door on a dollar bill. If the bill pulls out easily, you need a new gasket. A poor gasket lets warm kitchen air seep into your refrigerator which in turn lowers the efficiency of the appliance.

Cooking

• When making creamed vegetables for dinner, cook the vegies in the bottom of a double boiler and make the cream sauce, at the same time, in the top.

• Is your pilot light burning at peak efficiency? The flame should be blue with just a touch of yellow at the tip. If it is not, adjust the flame until it is.

• Your pots should be the same size or larger than the burner of your stove. Smaller-than-burner pots just waste fuel and two cups of water will boil faster in a larger pot anyway.

• When baking several items in your oven, stagger the pans to allow maximum circulation of air during cooking.

• For gas stoves, go over the burner holes with a wire brush several times a week. Clogged burner holes just waste gas.

• Whenever possible, make a complete meal in your oven.

• Dried fruits, beans and cereals cook in less time if they are soaked in water for several hours before cooking.

• To bake really large potatoes, cut them in half before putting them in the oven.

• Prefer your potatoes boiled? Rinse them in hot water before you start the cooking process. The potatoes will cook faster.

• So your favorite recipe says bake for thirty minutes. The last five or ten minutes, turn your oven off. The accumulated heat will finish the job. The average oven begins to lose heat after five or ten minutes.

• When boiling food, allow it to reach room temperature first. It cooks faster. This is true for frozen vegetables, too. Let them defrost first.

• A pinch or two of salt added to water will make it boil faster.

• No need to boil a whole kettle of water when you just want a cup or two. Measure the water into your kettle.

• Don't let sediment build up on the bottom of your kettle. It cuts down on the efficiency of the kettle.

Phoning

• Calling a relative long-distance? Keep a three-minute egg-timer by the phone. This way, you will know when you run into over-time.

• And another hint about long-distance telephone calls: Make a list of the things you want to discuss before dialing. If you do this, you won't have to call back because you forgot to relay an important tidbit of information.

• You can receive credit for wrong numbers. Just dial the operator, that's a free call, and give the number you reached in error. The operator arranges for credit so you won't be billed.

Heating

Fuel costs continue to rise. Here are a few pointers to keep you warm and snug at a lesser cost:

• Part of conserving fuel is an efficient heating system. Does yours need adjustment? Try this simple test: Hold a lighted cigarette near the floor in the middle of any room. If your heating system is efficient, the smoke will drift up or across the room slowly. If the heating system needs adjustment, the smoke will evaporate quickly or gather at one level.

• Drafts from doors, windows, and cracks can reduce your heating efficiency by as much as one-third. Each fall go over your house for "energy leaks" and seal them up.

• During the colder months, close off any rooms that you use rarely. Should you need the room for some reason, you can always re-open it temporarily.

• A cracked window pane allows heat to escape from your house.

• Do you really need that mail slot in your door? It does create a draft. Why not invest in an outdoor mailbox and seal the slot over with a piece of wood.

Electrical Appliances

• No one denies the need for electrical applicances, but they are expensive to operate. By using them at maximum capacity, you save money in the long run. So remember, run the washer, dryer, dish washer, even the toaster fully loaded. Think twice before running these units at less than full. As for your electric steam iron, have a good-sized pile to press. Using the iron for one or two pieces uses too much electricity.

• Many people like to leave the television set on when they go out to create the impression that someone is home. If you do, leave the radio rather than the television set on. A radio uses less electricity.

• You can reduce energy consumption if you pull down your win
dow shades or blinds at dusk and leave them down until morning
The air pocket that forms between the window and the shade or
blind forms a pretty good insulator. In the summertime, do just the
opposite; draw your shades or blinds during the daylight hours to
reduce the need for the air conditioner. Leave them up at night so
the cooler air can get in.

• A heated garage is a joy, but it does not have to be too heated
A temperature of 40°F is adequate.

Radiators

• Avoid blocking your radiators with furniture or piles of newspapers and magazines. The heat is cut off when you do. And make
sure your covered radiators are open enough at the bottom to allow
proper air circulation.

• Dark oil or water based paints are best for radiators.

• If you put a reflecting sheet behind your radiators, the heat will
be forced into the room and not absorbed by the wall.

• The cleaner the radiator, the more efficient it is. Vacuum your
radiators at least once a week.

• For really high radiator efficiency, take the covers off. Granted
this leaves what is basically an ugly fixture exposed, but you can always put the covers back on when you have guests.

Wood Stoves

Recently, interest in fuel conservation led many people to renewed interest in wood burning stoves. How about you? Does the
idea of stretching your fuel dollar with the use of a wood stove ap-
peal? If so, the following information could help you get the maximum efficiency and enjoyment from your stove:

• Fuel oil is sold by the gallon. Wood is sold by the cord. What's a
cord? As defined by law, one standard cord of wood is a pile four
feet high and eight feet long composed of sticks four feet in length.
Something known as a face cord is a pile of wood four by eight feet
composed of sticks of varying lengths. The sticks might be twelve,
sixteen, eighteen, or even twenty inches long. The amount of solid
wood in the stack varies according to the size of the sticks and the
straightness. Also, whether the sticks are round or split. Therefore,
a standard cord of wood may be made up of from sixty to 110 cubic
feet of solid wood.

• Another way of selling wood is by the weight or truck load.
Then it's hard to tell exactly how much wood you are getting

because there are so many variables like size of the truck, etc. If you must buy your wood this way, then make sure you are getting as much wood as possible. The wood should be dry. The signs of dry wood are loose bark and radial cracks.

• The best woods for burning, when seasoned, are hickories, oaks and locust. These woods are heavy so they give the most heat per cord.

• When you use a non-airtight stove, like a Franklin, you reduce your fuel efficiency by one-half.

• When burning wood, the combustion process is incomplete. This results in a build-up called creosote—unburned gases from the wood. You can reduce creosote build-up two ways: Make sure the wood you burn is as dry as possible, and stoke the hot fire daily for fifteen to thirty minutes.

CHAPTER 13

RECYCLING YOUR DISCARDS

We are rapidly becoming a nation of savers. "Broken" or "useless" objects are less likely to be thrown away than ever before. Mostly because it's becoming an expensive luxury. Been wondering how best to squeeze the last tidbit of use out of some household item past its prime? Here are a few ideas on how to regard a potential discard:

Nylons
Nothing goes faster than nylon stockings and panty hose and knee-highs. No sooner do you put them on when—you know—a run. How many pairs have you tossed into the garbage? Just because your hose develops a run, doesn't mean you can't get an extra run for your money.

• You can wrap a piece of nylon stocking around your baby's bottle. It provides a better grip, keeps the bottle warmer longer, and gives the baby a chance to learn a new "feel".

• Store plant bulbs in stockings. When stored this way, the bulbs can "breathe" freely.

• Cut a small hole in the toe of a stocking and use it as an umbrella holder. The umbrella will stay in shape longer—and cleaner, too.

• Old nylons make stuffing for cuddly toys. The nylon stuffing is easier to wash and dry.

• If you stretch a nylon stocking over a wire hanger, your clothes will not slip off as easily.

• Tired of moth balls rolling around in storage areas? Place the crystals in an old nylon stocking.

• Ruined stockings are great for tying up packages and bundles of newspapers. They stretch, bind and hold tight. They also have the advantage of being easier to handle.

• Need a mattress for your pet? Stuff old nylons into a pillow case and sew up the open end. This mattress is easy to wash. You can also stuff sagging chair seats and cushions with runny nylons.

• Don't know what to do with all those small bits and pieces of soap? Collect them in the toe of an old stocking. The nylon, with the soap chips, makes a dish scrubber—and it dries quickly.

• When you can't wear a stocking any longer, use it to strain used fats and oils.

• Need a clean head of hair but don't have the time for shampoo? Wrap your brush in a nylon and brush away. Any accumulated oil will be picked up by the nylon.

• That leaky hot water bottle can be stuffed with nylons and presto! A kneeling pad for gardening.

• For those who are allergic to wool, line the garments with old nylon stockings.

• Old nylons can be used in your drains to keep chunks of food, bits of hair, what have you, from clogging the drains.

New Life for Left-Overs

So much for nylon stockings. But here are some more recycling tips on just about everything. Nothing is to be thrown out the first time around.

• Bits and pieces of soap can be collected and run through your blender. Presto! Liquid soap.

• When the right-hand of your work glove is going thin, reverse both the right and left gloves. A new pair—almost.

• Worn out sheets, underwear and towels make great polishing rags. You can keep using them until they fall apart.

• The handles of old mops and brooms are good replacements for broken chair rungs.

• Missing the mate to a leather glove? Save the solo and use it to cover plain buttons. Leather buttons cost the earth today.

• Pillow cases can be made from old sheets. You can also use old sheets to make small tablecloths or crib sheets.

• Outgrown or overused raincoats can be cut up into waterproof covers for any article exposed to moisture. And talking about rubber, rubber gloves, when totally useless as hand protectors, can be cut into sturdy rubber bands.

• Don't toss out potato peelings. Let them dry and then burn them in your fireplace. This keeps the flue and chimney clean.

• Missing a knob from your potlid? Don't despair. Using a sharp-pointed screw, put it through the hole. Attach a cork. Presto, a potlid again. And best of all, the cork is heatproof.

• Old quilted robes and housecoats make sturdy pot holders and oven mitts.

• You can soften dried-out shoe polish by adding a drop or two of plain turpentine.

• Your hot-water bottles will last longer if you rub them with glycerin from time to time.

• Empty cigar boxes make excellent cartons for mailing small items. They also make good storage boxes for small items.

• Moving and want to protect your precious vases and crystal goodies? Use empty liquor cartons. The cardboard dividers make perfect separators to prevent knicks, chips, and cracks. And best of all, you can get the cartons for free from your local package store.

• Styrofoam egg cartons can be used as ice cube trays. And the oval-shaped cubes will intrigue your guests.

• The mesh bag used to package onions makes a good fresh vegetable scrubber.

• Worn-out curtains for standard-size windows can usually be cut down to make curtains for smaller windows, like the ones usually found in bathrooms, foyers and kitchens.

Left-Over Food

• Small servings of vegetables left over from a meal? Start collecting these small amounts all together. By the end of the week, you should have enough for a generous serving of mixed vegetables.

• Left over coffee and tea can be made into ice cubes and used for **iced** coffee and tea. These cubes provide a nice bit of extra flavoring.

• The juices and syrups drained from canned fruit can be used to baste roasted meats. The liquid can be stored in your refrigerator or frozen.

CHAPTER 14

HOUSEHOLD REPAIRS

More and more of us want to become do-it-yourselfers. Fortunately, there is no great mystery involved in making simple home repairs.

Tools

• To get the most from your sandpaper, dampen it slightly and secure it to a block with thumb tacks. The paper is easier to use this way and it also resists cracking.

• Plywood will not split if you apply a strip of masking tape at the point where you want to start cutting.

• Screwdrivers will not slip if you rub chalk at the tip.

• Nails can be driven into wood and walls more easily if you dip them in heavy lubricating oil—such as used for washing machines—first.

• To keep your tools from rusting, place a piece of white chalk or several mothballs in your toolbox. They both will absorb the moisture that causes the rust...or you can apply a coat of paste wax to your tools...or store them in a bucket of sand.

• Nonstick vegetable spray will silence squeaky hinges, loosen stubborn locks. It will also work well on roller and tricycle wheels.

Rust

• A rusted bolt will come loose if you apply a cloth soaked in the carbonated beverage of your choice...or apply a drop or two of household ammonia.

• To prevent rusting in the first place, wrap thread around the bolt and apply a thin coat of petroleum jelly before you add the nut.

Tool Use

• When you have to drive a nail through plastic, heat the nail first over a cigarette lighter. You will not split the plastic if you do this.

• When hammering a nail, support it with an old comb. This will prevent you from hitting your fingers accidentally.

• Whenever you are using pliers or a wrench, tape the ends so that you will not leave marks.

• Tired of slipping rulers and yardsticks. Coat the underside with soap and your measuring tools will stay put as you use them.

• And when you want to draw an accurate line on a piece of wood, use a pocket knife instead of a pencil.

• Suction cups adhere better when the surface to which they are to be attached is coated with soap.

• For more accurate drilling, start out with your smallest drill. And the drilling of hard metal will be easier if you lubricate the drill point with turpentine instead of oil.

• To help a hand saw go through a tight cut, apply a small quantity of kerosene.

Screws

• When dealing with screws, keep in mind that left is loose and right is tight. When a screw is so tight that you cannot undo, apply some peroxide with a cotton ball. Or heat the edge of the screwdriver over a cigarette lighter.

• For loose screws, insert a wooden match in the hole and break it off. Put the screw back in and tighten...or wind a few threads of steel wool around the screw threads...or you can apply fingernail polish to the screw and insert. When the polish dries it will act as an adhesive...or you can use paint or glue.

• To insert a screw for the first time, place a strip of cellophane on the wall. Take a nail and give it a few taps, just enough to make a "dent". Run the screw through a bar of soap and insert. The tape holds your wall in place and soap greases the process.

• When you have to replace a screw and can't take it with you, take the impression off to the hardware store. Take a piece of well-chewed gum and place it on a piece of waxed paper. Rub a dab of petroleum jelly over the gum. Flatten the gum slightly and press the screw down. There—a perfect impression that will allow you to make a perfect match.

• To keep the metal screws on your various appliances nice and tight, dab a drop of shellac under the heads before you tighten them.

• Having trouble storing all those screws and nails and nuts and bolts conveniently so you can find them again? Hammer the lids of jars to the beams of your basement or storage area. Sort out the household fasteners into each jar and screw onto the nailed lids. Keeps everything organized and handy.

Plumbing Tips

• Cold water pipes sweat more in the summer. Wrap the moist area with aluminum foil.

• Small water pipe leaks can be stopped temporarily with a leather belt. Secure the belt with wire; tighten the wire with a pair of pliers.

• To keep drains from stopping up, once a week pour a quarter pound of baking soda down. Slowly run boiling water in the drains.

• A clogged drain can be opened with a half cup of baking soda followed by a half cup of vinegar. Use a plunger to finish the job. If you do not have a plunger, cut a hollow rubber ball in half.

Walls

• You can locate the beams in your walls with a compass. The metal nails in the beam will cause a fluctuation in the compass.

• When you are spackling walls, add a few drops of the paint you will use when your sealing job is finished. This prevents any trace of spackle showing through the paint. When you are mixing dry spackle, add the paint first and then the water or the mixture will be too runny.

• For white walls that need repairing, apply a thick paste of flour and water. When the mixture dries, rub off the excess. The cracks and holes are covered and you don't have to repaint.

Plaster

• Another plastering without repainting hint: If you have some of the original paint left, add a few drops to the plaster. Keep adding until you achieve the desired shade. If you are out of the paint, use food coloring.

• Use white vinegar when mixing plaster. It won't dry out as quickly as it does with water. And for those hard-to-reach spots, use a rubber spatula—one of the very thin kind.

• For lumpless plaster, add the powder to the liquid, not the other way around.

• No more air bubbles when you fill small holes if you apply thinned out spackle with an eye dropper.

Legs

• To secure a loose chair leg, wrap the loose end with a tiny strip of nylon stocking or nylon thread. Apply glue. Reinsert the loose leg. You can also use a few drops of commercial wood expander.

• When a table leg is too short, place a teaspoon of Plastic Wood on a sheet of waxed paper. Press the short leg into the Plastic Wood until it matches the other three legs. Allow it to dry. Finish the job by trimming off the excess and sanding.

• Faucet washers can be used to fix a short table leg. Start out with one. Add more as necessary.

Making Do

• If a favorite vase springs a leak at the bottom, add a thin layer of melted paraffin. This repair job lasts indefinitely.

• Broken china can be repaired with clear nail polish. After the polish dries, the excess can be removed with—you guessed it—nail polish remover.

• The plastic lids from one pound coffee cans can be used to cover cans of oil and paint.

• When faced with the annoyance of a leaky faucet and there is no washer readily available, take a piece of good strong twine and wrap it around the pipe at the point where the washer belongs. Pull the twine really tight. This trick outlasts a commercial washer.

• When you have to mend broken glass, use melted alum. It is better than glue because it does not show.

• When you have to apply oil to hard-to-reach spots, an ordinary drinking straw makes a good funnel.

• After you have mended an object and are waiting for the glue to dry, set the object in modeling clay. This will secure the piece until the glue has dried. Then the clay will peel off easily.

• Since cellar floors, where most fuse boxes are found, tend to be damp, always stand on a rubber mat when changing a fuse.

• Nail rubber shoe lifts to the bottom of each ladder leg. This will make the ladder more secure. Glue a strip of sandpaper to each rung as this will give you better footing. And to save yourself banged shins, nail a piece of rubber to each rung. An old garden hose is perfect for this job. To prevent unsightly ladder marks on your walls, put a pair of socks over the top—the part that leans against the wall.

• The last place to put a throw rug is in front of a solid glass door. Someone could slip and go sailing through the glass.

• To avoid the possibility of fire in your workshop area, use an old plate. Upend a flower pot on the plate and drop your cigarette butts and matches through the hole. Any live sparks will be extinguished quickly.

Picture Hanging

• If your pictures won't stay straight, wrap some adhesive tape around the wire. The tape provides a more secure grip . . . You can also tack masking tape, sticky side out, around the back of the frame. Rehang the picture and press it against the wall.

• Before you start hammering picture hooks, decide exactly where you want your picture or mirror. Cut a piece of paper or cardboard the exact size of what you are planning to hang. Hold it against your wall until you find "The Spot".

• When you decide where the hanging will take place, mark the spot with an X. Place a piece of cellophane tape over the spot and bang away. You can also wet your fingertip to mark the spot on the wall. This leaves no mark on the wall or wallpaper.

• Have a plain picture frame but in no mood to refinish it? Ordinary liquid shoe polish will provide a lovely finish in a jiff. Apply two coats allowing each coat to dry thoroughly. Polish, to protect the stain, with clear paste wax. What color to use? Brown liquid polish gives wood a walnut tone while oxblood comes out like mahogany. Tan liquid polish dries to a light, warm maple color.

Ideas You Ought to Know About

• You can keep friction tape from unraveling at the edges if you cut an X on both sides of the roll. Do this with a single-edge razor blade.

• When you store lawn furniture away for the winter, wrap the pieces in those plastic garment bags you get from the dry cleaners.

• An empty plastic bleach bottle makes a great emergency scoop. Cut off the bottom of the bottle. Using a pair of scissors, cut away, in a curved line, about two inches of plastic. Do your cutting on the side of the bottle where the handle is.

• You can thaw out a frozen pipe with a hand-held hair dryer.

• Give all your shovels and trowels a good coating of spray wax. Dirt and snow and whatever will slide right off.

• When your rubber door stop looses its grip, roughen it up a bit with a piece of sandpaper.

• Want to dissolve old glue so you can undo a joint? Apply a liberal amount of white vinegar.

• For sticky drawers and windows, run a wax candle along the track. A bar of dry soap also does the trick.

• Think that you are done sanding? Check just to make sure. Run an old nylon stocking over the surface. If there are any rough spots left, the stocking will catch to them.

• You can splice cassette tapes back together with just a drop of nail polish remover.

CHAPTER 15

SMELLS AND ODORS

The quickest, easiest, and cheapest way to rid a room of an unpleasant smell (assuming that the source has been removed) is to open several windows and let nature take over. Unfortunately, sometimes the weather makes it difficult to rely on this "natural" method.

Kitchen Odors

• The most common kitchen odors, aside from cooking smells, come from foods generally stored in the open, like onions and potatoes. Never leave these foods in their original bags. Moisture tends to gather and that is what starts the spoiling process which is what causes the smell. Unbag onion and potatoes immediately and discard any that are soft. Store these foods in a cool, dry place—never under the sink.

• As for garlic, another odor-causing food, store it in the freezer compartment of your refrigerator. It will keep much longer. Frozen garlic is easier to chop and yet it defrosts quickly.

• For general kitchen deodorizing, boil six to eight cloves in one cup of vinegar. Continue boiling until the liquid is almost evaporated. MONEY-SAVING TIP: Vinegar is vinegar. Stay away from the fancy name brands. Buy either the store brand or the no-name brand. Or...

• Place two tablespoons each of sugar and cinnamon in a glass pie plate. Melt it slowly over a low heat. Or...

• Use dried orange peel in the same way. Or...

• Add a tablespoon of ground cloves to two cups of water and boil for fifteen minutes. Or...

• Keep a small bowl of vinegar near your stove. Your kitchen will always be fresh-smelling because the vinegar absorbs ALL odors. Replenish as the liquid evaporates.

FOOD ODORS

Brussel Sprouts, Cabbage, Cauliflower: While boiling, place a piece of white bread (the heel works well) over the vegetables. Cover the pot tightly. Or...

• Simmer a half a cup of vinegar on the stove while boiling the vegetables. MONEY-SAVING TIP: The vinegar, when cooled, can be returned to the bottle. Or...

• Add a tablespoon of vinegar for each cup of water you use when boiling the vegetables. The flavor of the food will not be affected.

Onion and Garlic: From cutting boards: Rub the surface with a damp sponge that has been sprinkled with a tablespoon of lemon or lime juice.

• From knives and cooking utensils (such as bowls): Rub the affected area with a slice of raw potato.

• From your hands: there are several methods given below. Whichever one you use, always wash your hands with cold water. Warm or hot water closes the pores of your skin to open and absorb the odor. Cold water, however, makes the pores tighten. After washing your hands, apply a liberal dose of your favorite hand lotion.

• Sprinkle your hands with celery salt before washing them. Or...

• Sprinkle your hands with lemon or lime juice before washing them. Or...

• Rub a teaspoon of prepared mustard over your hands before washing them.

Fish Odors: While baking, place half an apple in the pan.

To remove fish odors from:

Silverware: Add a teaspoon of dry mustard to the dishwater.

Chinaware: Add a teaspoon of vinegar to the dishwater.

Pots and Pans: Add half a cup of vinegar, cover, and boil for one minute. If you don't have the lid, place a piece of aluminum foil over the pot or pan.

Hands: Apply a tablespoon of lemon or lime juice to a damp sponge and wipe your hands all over. Wash your hands in cold water and apply a liberal dose of your favorite hand lotion.

Frying Odors: Place a cup of white vinegar near the stove while you are frying anything. Discard the liquid as it tends to absorb not only the odor, but also the oil itself.

Garbage Disposal Unit: Once a week, slice a lemon and grind it through the unit. Any time you are using lemons or limes, drop the peel into the unit last.

Garbage Cans (Indoors and Out): Once a week, wipe your garbage cans thoroughly with a sponge dipped in straight ammonia. Add one or two moth balls to each can. The mothball odor keeps insects away.

Drains: Once a week, flush each drain with boiling water. Put half a cup of baking soda down the drain. Flush with boiling water again.

MONEY-SAVING TIP: Buy either the store or no-name brand of baking soda.

Refrigerators: Place a piece of white bread, the heel will do nicely, in your refrigerator. Change once a week. And rather than throw the old bread away, crumble it and place it on your bird feeder. Or...

• Place half of a lemon in your refrigerator. Change once a week. Or...

• Place a tablespoon-sized ball of child's modeling clay in your refrigerator. Change once a month. Or...

• Saturate a cotton ball with vanilla extract and place it in your refrigerator. Change once a week. MONEY-SAVING TIP: Use either the store brand or no-name brand of extract.

Lunch Boxes: Sprinkle a liberal amount of baking soda on a damp sponge. Wipe the lunch box carefully. Rinse thoroughly in warm water. Dry and place in a sunny spot for a few hours.

Bathroom Odors: Keep a piece of activated charcoal near the toilet bowl. Or...

• Tape a sheet of fabric softener to the inside of the wastepaper basket. Change every week.

Throughout the House: To freshen any room quickly, place a bowl of vinegar on a table near the center of the room. Close the door and leave for about fifteen minutes. NOTE: After a party, remove the ashtrays. Place a bowl of vinegar in the room and shut the door. When you wake up, you won't have to enter a room reeking of stale smoke.

Paint and Varnish: To remove these odors from a china cabinet, slice an onion in half and leave one piece on the top shelf and the other on the bottom overnight. The onion will absorb the smell and not leave any behind.

• While painting, add two teaspoons of vanilla extract per quart of paint. Or...

• Slice an onion in half and place it, cut side up somewhere in the room while painting. Discard when done.

Closets and Drawers: To deodorize closets, mix a solution of equal parts of plain rubbing alcohol and lemon juice. Using a sponge or cloth, dip it in the solution, wring out well and wipe down the closet thoroughly. Leave the closet door open while it dries.

• To keep closets fresh, place a piece of activated charcoal on the floor or shelf. Replace every four to six weeks.

• To keep drawers smelling fresh, place two or three whole cloves in them.

CREATING PLEASANT SMELLS

• Using an atomizer, spray your favorite scent on the light bulbs. The heat from the bulbs will diffuse the scent throughout the room.

• There is no need to buy fancy solid room deodorizers. Make your own pomanders. They are not only easy to make, but they also last a long time. Pomanders offer a further advantage—they act as moth repellents.

To Make Orange Pomander: Take a fresh, firm-skinned orange (it is important that the fruit be fresh). Stud the orange liberally with whole cloves. The more you use, the better. Because the cloves are sharp, drive them into the orange while wearing a thimble. Wrap the orange in white tissue paper and store in a cool, dry, airy place for two weeks. Unwrap and place in a room or closet.

To Make Apple Pomander: Take a fresh, firm apple and stud with whole cloves. Preserve as you would the orange pomander. For a bit of extra color when using the apple pomander in a room, use a golden delicious apple. The contrast between the dark brown of the cloves and the bright yellow of the fruit is very cheery.

To Make Lemon or Lime Pomander: The process is the same as for the orange pomander. The ones made from lemon or lime are meant to be used in drawers and on the shelves of linen closets.

CHAPTER 16

HOUSEHOLD PESTS

Even the most fastidious housekeeper faces "The Uninvited" from time-to-time. Bugs, insects, household pests, whatever...you just can't avoid them all the time. Such problems are no reflection on your cleanliness. Rather it is a reflection on the persistence of the creatures. They are stubborn. There are, however, a few steps you can take to discourage them from dropping in. Here's how:

Prevention

• Keep all foods in clean, tightly sealed containers. Empty coffee cans with plastic lids make great containers. You can label each can with a piece of masking tape; this kind of tape peels right off when you want to use the can for something else. Large glass jars, with the original labels removed, also make great containers.

• If you save grocery bags and boxes for storage or garbage, give them a quick spray with a commercial bug killer. Insects are freeloaders, and they frequently hitch a ride home from the grocery store in bags and boxes.

• Plug holes in your screens as soon as you spot them. Airplane glue seals up small holes fast. And a piece of nylon netting makes a quick emergency screen.

• To keep bugs out of foods such as flour, corn starch or sugar, take a square of cloth, not cheesecloth, and a teaspoon of salt. Tie up the corners of the cloth, and keep it in the container with the vulnerable food. The salt does not change the flavor.

• Ants do not like the smell or taste of pine. Use a pine-sol disinfectant several times a week around your baseboards and window frame. If you hang your wash outside, spray your line and clothes pin bag frequently.

Okay, you've done your best; for all your hard work, you still find some sort of pest in your house. Now what? Try these helpful hints:

Ants

• Place small sponges soaked in sugar water wherever you see ants. Collect the sponges daily and pour boiling water over them.

• You can get rid of red ants by placing small quantities of green sage in the areas where they have been spotted.

• Ant hills outside your house can be destroyed by pouring a kettle of boiling water down each opening and then stepping on it to seal it off.

• You can sprinkle ordinary talcum powder around your doors and windows. Ants don't like to cross through talcum powder. Baking powder, salt and cayenne pepper also work quite well.

• Putting a few cloves in your cabinets and on your shelves will also keep ants down.

• To keep ants away from furniture, place coasters under the legs. Then add a teaspoon or two of pine disinfectant. Keeps your rooms smelling nice, too.

Cockroaches

• It takes only a one pound can of boric acid compound to keep your house free of these pests for at least a year. Boric acid does not kill roaches as rapidly as other pesticides, but it does last longer, and it is relatively safe. Roaches are not repelled by boric acid, so they keep going through it until they die. Sprinkle boric acid liberally in cracks, crevices, under sinks, and in all dark places.

• Any area where roaches gather can be coated with a mixture of lime, water, and a small quantity of salt. This will destroy the roaches in a few weeks time.

Flying Insects (Bees, Flies, Hornets, Wasps)

• Never mind insect sprays, they only make the bugs madder. Use hairspray instead. This stiffens their wings so that they cannot fly.

• Flies all over your garbage can? Hose them with disinfectant and then sprinkle soap powder in the bottom.

• Flying insect in your kitchen? Turn on the backdoor light and turn off the kitchen light. The "critter" will aim for the light, hit the backdoor and be struck by your swatter.

Mice

• Scatter mint leaves around the house, along your baseboards, on your shelves and in your cabinets.

• Never mind a better mouse trap, how about better bait? Mice love peanut butter. And you can add a ball of cotton to the trap. The mouse will try to snatch it for a nest.

• Balls of camphor placed in trunks, suitcases, cartons, drawers, under furniture, and such places will drive mice out.

Mosquitoes

• These pests breed in standing water. That means fishtanks, and

113

bowls of water under plants. Cover your fish tank with a fish net screen. What the fish don't eat, won't be able to escape. For plants that need constant dampness, forget the dish of water. Put a wet sponge under the plant. Just make sure to wet it every day.

Moths

• Notice moth holes in your favorite rug? Sprinkle the carpet with plain table salt and brush it in. After about an hour, vacuum the rug, and the moths and their eggs will go right into your vacuum cleaner.

Silverfish

• Sprinkle a mixture of boric acid and sugar on the affected areas.
• When washing articles that are to be stored, don't use starch as it attracts silverfish. They love the taste.

Termites

• You can prevent termites from ruining your wooden steps if you seal over the cracks with putty and then paint.

CHAPTER 17

HOME OFFICE UNITS

Life, we are told, keeps getting more complicated than ever before. Apparently so, because very few of us can run a house without some sort of "office space". The average household is something of a business. And to make the business of business that much easier, some ideas:

Mailing Tips

• When trusting breakables to the mails, you can reduce the chance of damage if you...wrap glass items in newspaper and put them in empty plastic-topped coffee cans. Make sure you use enough newspaper to keep the object from rattling around. Popcorn makes a good insulator for fragile items as do miniature marshmallows. This last one is especially good for cookies and such. And, too, the recipient can eat the marshmallows.

• When tying up a package, dampen the string first. As the string dries, it will become taut and, therefore, less likely to unravel.

• Afraid the address will disappear in inclement weather? Not to worry. When you have addressed a package, you can water-proof it by spraying the info with spray starch or hair spray...Or

by coating with clear nail polish...Or

by covering with cellophane tape.

• For addressing your packages in big, bold letters, dip a cotton swab in the ink.

• Out of glue and can't keep an envelope flap down? Try clear nail polish...or egg white.

• Unused stamps can be easily removed if they are held over a kettle of boiling water for a few minutes.

• When postage stamps stick together, stick them in your freezer for about thirty minutes. They will loosen quite easily.

• When you have a lot of envelopes to seal, run the flap over an ice cube...or dip a discarded nail polish brush in water. (And when you are finished with the bottle of nail polish, dip the brush in remover for a minute, rinse in warm water, and let dry.)

• Another tip for stuck together postage stamps: Cover them with a thin piece of paper, like onion skin, and run a warm iron over them.

• And another sealing tip: When you are finished with a bottle of rubber cement, wash both the bottle and brush thoroughly in warm, soapy water. Fill the jar with water and dip the brush in and moisten the glue on the envelope flaps.

• Cellophane tape, if stored in the refrigerator, will not stick. You will always be able to unroll it quite easily.

• And to remove cellophane tape from paper and cardboard, run a warm iron over it until it loosens.

Paper and Stationery

• Have a lot of papers to insert in your typewriter? To keep the edges straight, insert them in the flap fold of an envelope and then roll into your machine.

• If you have to staple a lot of papers together, the staple will be more secure if you lay a strip of cellophane tape on both the front and back and then staple.

• When you have to flip through a pile of papers, a little glycerin on your fingers will make the process that much easier.

• Mildew on important papers? No problem if you dust on a bit of cornstarch and leave it for several days. Brush off. If necessary, repeat the process.

Pens, Pencils and Erasers

• A clogged ballpoint pen will unclog if you hold the point over a match for a few seconds...a dip in boiling water also works well.

• You can remove ink by applying a bit of household bleach. Use a cotton swab, dip in the bleach, and erase away.

• For a quick pencil sharpening, use an emery board. Taping a board to the side of your desk makes using this trick a cinch.

• Erasers can be used to remove non-greasy smudges from paper.

Typewriters

• To keep your hands absolutely clean while changing a ribbon, wear a pair of those thin surgical gloves available in drug stores.

• Typewriter keys can be cleaned quickly and easily, and cheaply with nail polish remover...or rubbing alcohol. A cotton swab is ideal for this job and both fluids evaporate fast.

• Once your baby outgrows the need for a rubber sheet, wash it well and use it as a pad for your typewriter. You can fold it as thick as you like.

And Finally

• Save the pieces of cardboard that you find in packages of typing paper. They come in handily when mailing photographs or anything else that should not be bent or folded.

• Newspaper clippings will stay readable longer if you glue them to file cards and then wrap in plastic wrap.

• Desk drawers do not have to be pulled for a good cleaning. The radiator attachment of your vacuum cleaner is perfect for the job.

• Leather briefcases and attache cases will last longer if they are given a thin coat of furniture wax and polished with a soft cloth.

CHAPTER 18

PLANTS AND FLOWERS: REAL AND ARTIFICIAL – INDOOR AND OUT

There's nothing like flowers and plants to give color to what otherwise might be rather drab area. Lots of people feel this way but give up on flowers and plants before they even start. "No green thumb," they claim. Are you one of them? Well, these tips can go a long way toward giving you a green thumb. And if you've already got one, they may help to turn your thumb even greener!

Watering and Nourishing

• Your dishwasher and laundry equipment can do double duty for plants that thrive in humidity. When using these machines, move your humidity-loving greenery nearby. Better yet, brighten up your kitchen and laundry area with such plants.

• Cacti and succulents thrive on egg shells. Crush them and mix with the soil. Because the shells are alkaline based, they add calcium that these plants require.

• When watering any indoor plant, make sure the water is at room temperature. Cold water can "shock" the root system. And if your water supply is chlorinated, let the water stand for twenty-four hours so the added chemical will evaporate. Chlorine may be good for your teeth, but it is not good for your plants.

• Can't tell if your plants need a watering? Poke your finger about one inch into the soil. If it feels damp, no water necessary.

• When you boil eggs, let the water cool and use it for your plants. It has more minerals than a vitamin pill. You can also drop egg shells into a jar of water for a day and then use the liquid for your plants.

• Flat club soda is great for plants, too.

• Bulb-type plants should be watered from the bottom up. Place them in a shallow saucer and add the water to that.

• A small, portable vaporizer can be used to add moisture to a room with a lot of plants.

• Melted snow at room temperature is good for watering purposes.

• Find watering a messy job? Get yourself a small funnel and insert it into the soil. Pour the water slowly through the funnel.

• Your flowering plants not blooming? Then add a birth control pill to a quart of water, water liberally and watch the results.

118

Everything...including African violets...will burst into flower. It's the estrogen the plants go for.

• Ferns benefit from a teaspoon of castor oil or two tablespoons of olive oil every three or four months.

• Tea at room temperature is good for ferns, especially ones that seem to be a bit wilted.

• Ferns also get benefit from an occasional watering of a very weak ammonia solution. The nitrogen is what helps them.

• A raw onion placed at the bottom of a fern pot keeps the plant looking lively. Worms in your ferns? Stick matches, heads down, into the soil. The sulphur chases the worms.

•

Cleaning

House plants have to be kept dusted because the dust blocks the sunlight. To keep your plants clean, try these tips:

• Sponging the leaves with milk gives a nice shine.

• A few drops of mineral oil on a piece of cotton is good, too...so is beer...and petroleum jelly...or baby oil...or glycerine.

Grow Your Own

• A peach pit, planted one inch deep in a pot of soil, will grow long, thin, willow-like leaves. It looks very tropical.

• Place an avocado pit in fresh water until it sprouts. Then transfer it to a pot with the point up.

• Place a pineapple top in a jar of water with the prickly part down. When roots appear, put it in a flower pot.

• If you sprinkle a moist sponge with parsley and leave it near a window, you'll soon have nice green leaves.

Cuttings

• You can start your own plants, either for your own windowsill, for gifts or even for sale, by merely snipping off a branch or cutting from the following plants, putting in a glass of water and then planting in soil in a pot once the roots form. The plants that grow easily and profusely with this method are Swedish ivy, begonias, wandering jew, arrowhead, pothos, philodendron, oleander, pandanus and English ivy. Some have even had success at growing African violets with this method. The beauty of this procedure, of course, is that you can take cuttings from the cuttings once they've bloomed into healthy plants and ad infinitum.

119

Plant Problems

• To revive ailing plants, place a pest strip around the plant and cover it with a plastic bag. The bag should cover the plant completely. In a few days, you're plant will be perky again.

• A broken stem can be splinted with a toothpick and held in place with thread.

• Narrow strips cut from old plastic bread bags are great for tying plants.

• A sliding curtain rod, a small one, can be placed in the flower pot and the plant secured to it. As the plant grows, you just pull the rod up to the appropriate height.

• While tying a plant, you can hold the stem in place with a snap clothespin.

• Need a trellis in a hurry? Snap the hook off a wire hanger and bend the rest into a pleasing shape.

• If you line the inside of any metal planter with aluminum foil, the planter will not rust.

• Want to paint your flower pots? Place the pot over a tin can turning the can as you paint.

Should your plants be pestered by pests, here are a few tips for getting rid of the bugs:

• For aphids and spiders, wash the whole plant off with a mild detergent mixed in water.

• For black flies, mix two tablespoons of plain household ammonia with one quart of water. Water your plants with this solution.

• For slugs, put the plant in a pot of clear water. For pests in general, stick a clove of garlic into the soil. As it sprouts, push the clove down into the soil or cut off the growth.

Vacation Watering

• Going away and don't want your plants to be thirsty? No need to call on friends. Submerge bricks in your bathtub and fill with water until the bricks are just covered. Rest the plants on the bricks. You can also use thickly folded bath towels or even newspaper for the same results.

• Another neat trick is to take a length of clothesline, bury one end in the soil and leave the other in a pail of water. The pail must be higher than the flower pot.

• For short trips away, just leave the plants in saucers of water. You can also insert a small funnel into the soil and fill it with water. The moisture will be released one drop at a time.

Cut Flowers

And for cut flowers, here are ways to make them last longer than ever before:

• Always cut your roses just before the buds turn soft. Use a sharp knife to trim the ends of roses and most flowers. Scissors tend to crush the stems.

• Chrysanthemum stalks and other woody branches should be broken off and crushed. Thick stems should be split.

• After trimming, dip the stems into warm and then cold water. This will cause the stems to expand and therefore absorb more water.

• Never crowd cut flowers into a vase. They need room to breath.

• A drop or two of melted wax in the centers of tulips will keep them from opening wide. You can also put a copper penny in the water.

• Remove all leaves that rest below the waterline. Rotting leaves poison the water.

• For short-stemmed flowers, a bowl of well-watered sand is best.

• Two ounces of glycerin added to the water for autumn leaves will keep them fresher longer.

• Add a bit of sugar to water used for chrysanthemums. Carnations do well with boric acid.

• For making the flowers last longer, add activated charcoal or aspirin tablets or ice cubes or a teaspoon of white sugar to each pint of water. Or try adding weak tea or a teaspoon of salt or a thin slice of soap to the water.

• Refrigerate cut flowers overnight and change the water daily. Be sure to wash out the vase thoroughly.

• Keep cut flowers away from drafts or heat—especially keep them off the television set.

• Geraniums love coffee grounds. And violets do well when watered with dissolved birth control pills.

• Wilted flowers will revive temporarily if placed in hot water then put them in a dark place until the water is cool. After treatment, they should be transferred to cold water.

• You can tint white flowers by adding ordinary food coloring to the water.

• Remove the tight buds from your gladiolas. They really don't open and their weight causes the top blossoms to sag.

• Rosebuds open faster when you add a lump of sugar to the water.

• Short-stemmed flowers can be arranged with long-stemmed ones if you use ordinary drinking straws for the shorties.

• Rollers, tied together, make great flower holders.

• Fresh fruits and vegetables should be kept away from fresh flowers. Fruits and vegies give off ethylene gas which is harmful to flowers.

• To really preserve flowers and leaves, hold a can of hair spray about twelve inches back and spray.

Winter Flowers

• You can have fresh flowers from your own garden even in winter. Prune twigs or branches from forsythia, crab apple, hawthorn, lilac—any flowering tree or shrub. Put the branches in a bucket of warm water and add a cotton ball soaked in ammonia. Cover the pail and the branches with a plastic bag—like the ones you get from dry cleaners. The fumes from the ammonia will force the twigs and branches to blossom like spring.

• How about drying your own flowers and leaves for all-year-round color in your home? Here's how: Mix together ten parts white cornmeal and three parts borax. Bury your flowers in this for two weeks. Another way, hammer the ends of the branches or the stems. Stand in a jar containing a solution of two-thirds water and one-third glycerin. The solution should reach three or four inches. If you like, you can just lay the flowers in this liquid. In a week or so, the solution will be absorbed. A slight color change often takes place using this method.

Artificial Flowers

When fresh flowers and plants are not avilable, or not desirable, the perfect compromise is the artificial variety. One obvious advantage to artificial plants and flowers is that they last "forever" and require very little care.

• For dust-free artificial flowers, brush them with absorbent powder. Don't like the powder idea? Then dust your artificial flora once a week to keep them fresh looking indefinitely.

• To clean plastic flowers, put one-quarter cup of salt in a paper bag and add the flowers. Shake vigorously.

• Want to give your plastic flowers a bath? Use a worn-out toothbrush, warm water and mild soap.

• Porcelain flowers can be swished in a mild solution of household ammonia, detergent and warm water. For hard to reach areas, use an old toothbrush. Rinse in clear, warm water and lay on paper towels until dry.

• To keep artificial flowers from flopping around in the vase, pour a generous helping of common table salt into your vase and add just enough water to moisten the salt. Arrange your flowers. When the water evaporates, the salt will harden and hold the posies in place. When you want to remove the flowers, pull them out gently and add enough warm water to loosen the salt. Then rinse the vase out thoroughly.

• Artificial and dried flowers stay fresh looking when sprayed with hair spray. You can also coat your artificial flowers with clear nail polish.

• Your artificial flowers really looking bedraggled? You can perk them up again by dipping them in silver or gilt paint. For extra flash, add a few sparklers while the paint is still damp.

• Artificial fruits should be washed in mild soap and warm water and dried well. A thin coat of petroleum jelly will give the fruit a shiny, natural look.

• Wax fruit responds well to a quick wipe with rubbing alcohol.

OUTDOOR GARDENING

The great outdoors requires tools for gardening. And they need just as much care as your plants, flowers and lawn. So here's how to keep yourself all tooled up:

Garden Tools

• Don't have one of those fancy holders for your garden hose? An old, leaky galvanized bucket can be used. Nail the bucket, through the bottom, to any solid surface—your garage wall, the side of your house—and coil the hose around it.

• The wooden handles on your garden tools won't warp if you occasionally wipe them with linseed oil.

• Garden tools should be cleaned when you're done using them. Hardened earth and dirt can be removed by soaking in hot, sudsy water. Dry them and coat with paste wax...or non-stick pan spray...to keep the grime from sticking in the future.

• Or you can clean your tools by dipping into a bucket of sand which has been moistened with oil. The sand-dip helps to keep the edges sharp, too.

• To prevent rust from forming, wrap metal tools in clear plastic. But if rust does appear, rub it away with a steel wool pad dipped in kerosene...or a corn dipped in olive oil.

• Tired of lending your tools and never seeing them again? Paint your initials on the handle. That will remind the borrower!

• Shoe bags make great holders for small garden tools.

• And so you won't lose your tools amid the grass and flowers of your garden, wrap brightly colored tape—red, yellow, orange—around the handles.

• For those of you who still use a lawn mower, the blades will stay sharper longer if you wipe them with an oily cloth after each use.

• For your power mower, a plastic dry cleaner's bag makes a great protective wrapper.

• If you mark your garden spade in inches or feet, you'll immediately know how far down you've dug.

• When storing your tools for the winter, wash your hose down with soapy water and dry; clean your sprayer with a solution of three tablespoons baking soda to a quart of warm water, and apply a thin coat of shellac to your metal items. Everything will be ready for you in the spring and no expense for replacements.

Weeds

• To dig out weeds and dandelions, use an apple corer. It gets to the roots without harming nearby plants. Gasoline also destroys dandelions.

• Place some grass seed in a screw-top jar. Punch a few holes in the top. As you weed the lawn, sprinkle on grass seed.

• For poison ivy, spray the vine with a solution of three pounds of table salt in one gallon of soapy water. Two or three good soakings will kill the ivy.

• For weeds and grass growing between cement sidewalks, pour salted boiling water over the growth. To keep the weeds and grass down, sprinkle salt over the area...Or use a cheap grade of motor oil. It works just as well.

Garden Pests

• Birds nibbling your freshly planted grass seed? If before planting you soak the grass seed overnight in liquid bluing, you will discourage your feathered friends. Birds dislike the taste of the bluing, but the seeds remain unharmed.

• But never mind birds, what about the rabbits? Here's an easy-to-make gadget that will keep the cottontails away. Take an aluminum pie plate and bend one side down and the other side up. Using a thumb tack, pin the plate to a sturdy stick. Don't push the tack in too tightly—the plate should be loose enough to turn easily in the wind. Drive the stick into the earth close by the endangered plants. The spinning plate and the reflection will send the rabbits scooting off.

• ...And rabbits don't like talcum powder. Sprinkle a little around the edge of your garden.

• They also hate the smell of moth balls. You can scatter a few around. As the balls or flakes melt, replace them.

• Moth balls and flakes also keep dogs and cats away from plants.

• Another way to discourage the neighborhood cats and dogs from congregating in your garden: Mix a pine-based household cleaner, four tablespoons to a sprinkling can of water. Use this solution about twice a week on your plants and shrubs. The mix will not harm your plants, but the aroma of the pine oil keeps dogs and cats away.

Insecticides a la Naturelle

For those of you who want to avoid the use of chemical insecticides, here's a list designed by nature herself:

• Herbs of all kinds will repell insects of all kinds. Always plant herbs among your plants and flowers.

• Basil by tomatoes keeps worms and flies away.

• Mint, sage, dill and thyme keep the cabbage moth away from vegetables like cabbage, cauliflower, broccoli and Brussel sprouts.

• Anise and coriander repel aphids.

• To keep the potato beetle off your spuds, plant horseradish in between the rows.

• Sometimes one plant can help another. Onions and garlic should be planted near carrots and beets. Japanese beetle, carrot flies and aphids do not like onions or garlic. Onions also serve the same purpose for lettuce and beans of all kinds.

• Radishes planted close to cabbage will keep down maggots.

• As a general rule of thumb, a row of vegetables around your garden will keep bugs at a minimum. Vegetable roots secrete an oil which the most common garden pests find offensive.

• For general all around spraying, use soap suds. This makes a cheap and effective insecticide which does not harm growing things.

• Remember, some vegetables do not like each other. Peas should never be planted near garlic. Onions should never be planted near strawberries. The aroma from the vegatable affects the fruit.

Hints for Healthy Soil

• A border of clam shells provides your garden with needed calcium. Mixing crushed egg shells into the soil does, too.

• Save your coffee grounds and tea leaves. Work them into the soil. It's a great way to increase the acid level where necessary.

Hints for the Gardener

• To keep dirt out from under your fingernails, scrape your fingers along a bar of dry soap. When you are done with your gardening, the dirt and grime will wash away quite easily.

• An old leaky hot water bottle makes a terrific outdoor kneeling pad.

• Ordinary cuticle remover will take grass stains off your hands.

• If you cut the cuffs off gardening pants, you won't clog your washing machine or drains with grass cuttings and dirt and such.

• And for general hand cleaning after gardening, nothing works like ordinary baking soda. Sprinkle some on your hands and moisten. Rub lightly and rinse. This method leaves your hands softer than the standard hand cleaning compounds which are quite harsh.

Planting and Transplanting Hints

• Where to start your plants? Empty ice cream cups are great. What is more, when the seedling is ready for a permanent home, you can put the cup right into the ground. In a few weeks, the cup will disintegrate.

• The plastic containers used for yogurt, cottage cheese and sour cream are also very good to use when starting plants.

• Another excellent container—plastic egg cartons. For paper egg cartons, they, too, can be placed directly into the soil.

• Small plants need reinforcement. Use empty plastic bottles. Just cut off the tops and the bottoms. Then stick them into the soil. When the plant is mature enough to stand on its own, you can cut the bottle along the side and remove.

• Coffee cans, with the bottoms cut out, are good supports for very young tomato plants. After a few weeks, remove the can.

• Discardable panty hose and nylon stockings are very useful for tying up stems and such. The nylon is less harsh.

• Clip clothes pins are very useful when cutting roses. Clip the pin to the stem and cut. This reduces your changes of getting scratched.

• Need a hotbed? A child's wagon does quite well. Fill with soil, plant your seeds and cover with a sheet of glass. When you are ready to transplant, you can transport your garden easily, too.

• An apple corer is ideal for transplanting.

• Want to start plants such as roses from cuttings? Make a hole in a raw potato. Insert the cutting and then plant as usual. This method allows the cutting sufficient moisture to put down strong, healthy roots.

• Do your plants need protection from frosty night air? Empty milk cartons—both quart and half gallon size—with the tops cut off can be used as protective covers.

• To keep your plant markers from being ruined by the rain these methods work equally well for seed packets and for commercial tags: Dip them into melted wax. . .or coat with clear nailpolish. . .or wrap them in plastic sandwich bags. If you don't care to use a whole plastic bag, you can cut off pieces to size for your tags. Secure with staples or with the ties used on loaves of bread.

• Love fresh vegetables from your garden but hate to rinse them off in your sink? Make an outdoor sieve. An old screen or a piece of screening nailed to a frame is what you want. Place your vegetables on this and clean them off with your garden hose. The nozzle should be set on the fine spray.

CHAPTER 19

AUTO ADVICE

The automobile changed our lives. But for most women, and a goodly number of men, too, the family car remains a mystery. When it works well, when the engine purrs along, we love our cars. Let the opposite happen—the car stalls in traffic and refuses to start, smoke pours from under the hood—and we hate our cars. Many auto problems and emergencies can be avoided. The secret is preventive maintenance. What follows are some suggestions anyone can use because getting the most from your automobile does not mean you have to be a master mechanic.

Conserving Gasoline

• When out shopping for a new car, bear in mind that the lighter the car, the less power it takes to move it. And the less power required, the less gasoline you use. Think about that before you decide on an engine size.

• Starting and stopping your car burns a lot of gasoline, far more than a long, steady drive. To keep your gasoline costs under control, combine several errands into a single trip.

• While driving at fifty-five miles per hour conserves gasoline, driving at less than twenty-five wastes gas.

• Save your air-conditioning for really hot days. On warm days use the ventilation system.

• Should you find yourself running low on gas, don't speed up. Slow down to conserve what you have left.

Auto Safety First

• Keep the owner's manual in your glove compartment. Should you have a breakdown on the road, the manual won't do you much good if it's home in a desk drawer.

• Unless you store valuables in your glove compartment, leave it unlocked. Should someone break into your car, they won't have to jimmy the glove compartment open to pinch a road map.

• Unless state law requires otherwise, carry your automobile registration and insurance card on your person. Many people tend to leave these items in their glove compartments. Should a thief get into your car, a registration and insurance card tells him two things (1) Where you live—for future reference—and (2) That you are not home at the present moment.

• In a pinch, very few of us know the serial number of our car. For emergency proof of ownership, write your birth date on a 3x5 card and drop it down a window slot. Even if an unauthorized individual finds the card, that vital statistic won't get them far.

• Carry your medical history in terms of allergies and blood type with you in case of accident. Type this information on a 3x5 card and clip or staple it to your driver's license.

• If you place a layer of baking soda or sand in the ashtrays of your car, cigarettes won't smolder.

• A frozen lock can be defrosted very quickly and easily. Heat the key over a cigarette lighter for a few minutes. Just remember, don't try to force the lock. It will open with a gentle turn.

• Do you find that you cannot locate your car in crowded parking lots? Try painting a piece of metal with luminous paint. When you leave your car, lay the metal on the dash board. Reflections from the sun or parking lot lights will guide you back. You can also attach a distinctive pennant to the antenna of your car.

• Carry an extra ignition/door key in your wallet. You'd be surprised the number of people who lock their keys in the car.

Summer Car Care

• During the summer, don't apply too much wax to the hood of your car. While driving, the glare from the sun can reflect back into your eyes and prove a driving hazard.

• Since heat causes gasoline to evaporate faster, whenever possible park your car in the shade. And keep the gasoline level in your fuel tank as high as possible. When there is little gasoline in the tank, there is more room for evaporation.

• Because of the higher temperatures, batteries need more checking in the summer than in the winter. Check your battery at least two times a month during hot weather to make sure there is no evaporation.

• When you park your car on a hot day, leave the inside air vents, and not the windows, open. An open window makes it too easy for people to get into your car.

Winter Car Care

• To keep locks from freezing, seal them with masking tape. This prevents moisture from getting into the locks. You can also put a little lubricating oil or graphite into the locks. Both are moisture retardents.

- In the winter, don't fill your radiator up to the top. Leave room for antifreeze expansion.
- You can prevent the doors and truck lid of your car from freezing in winter. Give the rubber gaskets a heavy coating of cooking oil. The oil will act as a water repellent, the major cause of freezing, and will not damage the gasket. This trick is especially good before a wintertime car washing.
- Car won't start on a cold morning? Don't yell for a mechanic until you try this one: Using an electric hair dryer, blow hot air on the carburetor. In nine cases out of ten, this gem works.
- Salt residue on automobile carpeting is ruinuous. Every few weeks during the cold, salty months, go over the carpeting in your car with a solution of one part warm water to one part white vinegar. A sponge is the perfect applicator.

Cleaning Your Car

- The best way to wash your car is with a solution of one cup of kerosene to a bucket of warm water. The kerosene does wonders. You don't have to wet the car down first, and you don't have to rinse it off. And the next time it rains, the water drops will bead off.
- A quick wipe-down with a few drops of kerosene will remove gas spills from around your fuel tank, too.
- If the hood of your car doesn't look as shiny as the rest of the body, give the underside of the hood a coat of aluminum paint. This treatment will deflect sun glare which is what causes the wax and polish to melt.
- Never wipe dust or dirt from your car with a dry cloth. This action can cause scratches.
- Put a little olive oil in the car wash water. Dirt and grime will come off more easily.
- Keeping your car clean is very important. Dirty cars, especially dark colored ones, are more difficult to see during the night or in bad weather.
- Whenever you use cleaning solvents on the inside of your car, do the job with the car doors open. Many of those cleaning fumes are dangerous if you breath them in for too long a period of time.
- You can remove old bumper stickers with nail polish remover or lighter fluid. As the sticker softens, scrape it away with a single edged razor blade.
- The price tags adorning your new car can be removed if you apply hot vinegar. Keep sponging on the vinegar until the sticker loos-

ns. You can also use lemon extract the same way. Or you can smear the tag with salad oil. Leave it for a while and then scrape off with a single edged razor blade.

• Scratches can be masked with ordinary crayon.

• Sometimes a small dent will come out if you force a plunger against the damaged area. The pressure from the suction can restore the section dented.

• Pieces of old carpets are terrific polishing cloths for your car.

• Line the bottom of your trunk with a piece of linoleum and keep it waxed. Not only does this protect the trunk floor, but it also makes sliding tools in and out much easier.

• To keep your new car's chrome fittings shiny, apply a coat of clear lacquer. You can keep the chrome looking brand new if you polish it with clear furniture wax.

• When you do get rust spots on the chrome, scrub the area briskly with a piece of aluminum foil which has been crumpled...or scrub with a steel wool soap pad...rub on a little kerosene. Water and similar stain spots can be removed from chrome with plain lemon juice.

Tar Spots

• Tar can be removed with linseed oil, the raw kind. Apply the oil and allow it to stay until the tar is soft. Using a clean cloth which has been dampened with linseed oil, wipe the tar away. Ordinary cooking lard works in much the same way. So does a solution of one cup of kerosene to one gallon of warm water.

• For tar spots on chrome, sprinkle baking soda on a damp cloth and rub away. The baking soda will not scratch the chrome.

Skunk

• Should you ever have car contact with a skunk, you can get rid of the lingering aroma this way. Dissolve one cup of dry mustard in a bucket of warm water. Slosh this solution on the parts of the car that need it. Repeat until the scent is gone.

Tires

• Whenever you add air to your tires, check the spare, too.

• When putting a tire on a new rim, smear the inner edge, or bead, of the tire with soapy water. This will serve as a lubricant thereby making the whole process quicker and easier.

• White-walls do not take well to scouring powders or steel wool pads. They scratch the rubber. Clean your white walls with a damp sponge and baking soda. If the whites are really dirty, use a stiff, but not a wire, brush. To keep your white-wall tires from becoming dirty in the first place, wipe them down once a week with a bucket of warm soapy water to which a quarter cup of lemon juice has been added.

Windows and Windshields

• If your visor does not provide enough relief from the glare of the sun, you can add more. Secure a manila envelope to the visor with a rubber band.

• An old shower curtain makes a great windshield protector for those times when it looks like snow. So do pads of old newspapers. In the morning, all you have to do is remove the covering. Pieces of cardboard secured under the wipers also work well.

• Your windshield wipers will last much longer if you first turn them on at the lowest speed. You can speed them up after the windshield is completely wet. This way, the friction from dust and dirt does not harm the blades.

• When you think you may run into rain, apply moistened baking soda to your windshield wipers. This method keeps the window clear.

• If your windshield wipers are not up to par, rub them gently with a sandpaper block—fine sandpaper. This will clean and smooth them.

• The plastic net onion bags make excellent car window cleaners. The plastic really gets off sap, dead bugs and bird stains.

• If you rub moist salt on your windshield, inside and out, the window will not frost up. A cut onion and tobacco from a cigarette butt will have the same effect.

• A small amount of baking soda sprinkled on a damp sponge will remove even the toughest dirt and grime from your windshield.

• Linen, the older the better, is the best polishing cloth for car windows. And never use the same cloth to do the windows that you used to do the body of the car. You can easily transfer wax and other undesirables to your car windows.

• Keep a whisk broom, blackboard eraser or long handled brush in your car to remove snow easily and quickly.

• You can make your windshield wiper solvent. Add one quart of rubbing alcohol, one cup of water, and two tablespoons of liquid detergent. Shake well. This mixture will not freeze at temperatures above 35°F.

Safe Driving

• While driving in winter with the heater going, leave at least one window open a quarter of an inch.

• The faster you drive, the less you can see. When you do seventy miles per hour, your vision is just half of what it would be if you were doing forty.

• By changing the stations on your car radio during long drives, you can help prevent drowsiness. And in rainy, snowy weather, the sound of your windshield wipers can have a hypnotic effect. Vary the speed from time to time.

• On long drives a cola drink laced with a teaspoon of salt will revive you for a bit.

• After you've tinkered with your car's battery, rinse your hands in a solution of water and baking soda. This will neutralize any acid you may have picked up while in contact with the battery.

• Keep a good, strong rubber band in the glove compartment of your car—along with a flashlight. Should you ever be stuck, you can use the rubber band to fasten the flashlight to a holder while you work.

• A box of baking soda in the glove compartment makes a perfect fire extinguisher for an engine fire. Should your engine catch on fire, turn off the ignition and sprinkle a liberal dose of soda over the flames.

• If you have a roll of reflector tape in your car, you can put on strips if a head or tail light burns out suddenly.

• While a raised hand is the universal signal for a road emergency, a white handkerchief tied from the handle of the driver's door serves to underscore the fact help is needed.

Problem Solvers

• Keep a couple of empty milk cartons in the trunk of your car. They make fine emergency flares and burn for as long as fifteen minutes.

• Have a pot holder in your car. If you ever have to remove the radiator cap, the holder will keep you from burning your hands.

• While sand makes fine traction, it is heavy. Kitty litter is much lighter and works just as well. So do pieces of old carpeting. Should you become stuck and find yourself without sand, litter, or carpeting, the rubber mats from your car floor can help greatly.

• Should your bumper become locked to another, try placing a heavy board or even a log directly behind the front wheels. Back up slowly. The board often raises the front end of a car just enough to unlock the bumpers.

• Jumper cables are a must for every driver. Remember, hook the red cable to the positive side of the battery of the car that is running. The other red cable is hooked to the positive side of the car that is NOT running. The black cables are hooked to the negative posts in any order. If you can't read the markings, the positive post is always the one that is larger.

• When buying a fire extinguisher for your car, select one that is the dry-chemical type...nonfreezing and one that you can use on oil, grease and electrical fires. From time to time, check the extinguisher to make sure it is fully charged. And keep it somewhere in the car that is handy to both driver and passenger.

• Make a point of keeping your license plates clean and waxed. They are meant to identify your car, and if you are ever stuck, a dirty, unreadable plate could result in your being described as just another disabled vehicle.

• An inexpensive shoe bag attached to back of the front seat of your car is a great storage area for maps, cigarettes, small toys, even your gloves and scarves.

An Ounce of Prevention...

• Car tools tend to rust when stored in the trunk. To prevent this, paint the tools with a rust-retarding paint.

• When going on a long trip, take the tools and spare tire out and then add the luggage. Replace the tools and tire. This way, should you need them, they are handy. You don't have to haul out all the heavy bags first.

• Backing into your garage is better. This way, if your car won't start, you can use jumper cables more easily.

• Have trouble judging the area in your garage? Suspend a rubber ball from the ceiling. When it hits your rear window (or windshield, if you park front end first), you will know that you are in far enough.

Motor Maintenance

• When you suspect you have an oil leak but are not sure, spread a layer of clean newspaper under the front end. Then start the engine and run it for several minutes at a low of twenty to twenty-five miles. If you see oil on the newspaper when you turn the engine off, then you have an oil leak.

• When you hear a squealing sound as you turn the steering wheel, it means your steering belts are loose. Have them tightened immediately.

- The regular user of a car can rarely tell when the brakes need tightening. Mark the support of your brake pedal with dots of red nail polish. Use the side of the support toward the passenger side. When you have a passenger, ask how many dots are showing after you step on the brakes. If too few remain visible, have your brakes checked.

- One of the major causes of breakdowns on the road is broken hoses and belts. Keep an eye on them. Give each hose a good squeeze. If it seems soft and mushy, have it replaced. Snap the belts. Again if it seems flexible, have them replaced.

- Steel wool is excellent for securing a loose tail pipe. Saturate the steel wool with rust repellent before.

- To remove oil stains from your garage floor, saturate the stain with pine disinfectant. Scrub hard with a stiff brush and leave for twenty minutes to half an hour. Hose down the floor.

CHAPTER 20

CHILD CARE

These suggestions do not remove completely the problems of child care. They do, however, reduce them to a more manageable level.

Bath Time

• If you wear an old cotton glove on your left hand when bathing your baby, he won't slip from your grasp. If you're lefthanded, then wear the glove on your right hand.

• Is your baby too big for an infant tub but not quite big enough for the bathtub? Use one of those open work plastic laundry baskets as a tub within a tub...or you can use an infant seat. Remove the pad and buckle strap. Line the seat with a bath towel. And, place a towel on the bottom of the tub. This second towel will keep the infant seat from slipping and sliding.

• When children are old enough to bath themselves, put the bar of soap in an old white sock. This arrangement provides a better grip for small hands.

• If you are out of mild baby shampoo, you can still prevent stinging eyes. Rub a small amount of petroleum jelly on each eye lid.

• Plastic cups and dishes make nice bathtime toys.

• Small babies are sometimes terrified when given their bath. Wrapping the baby in a terry towel before immersing in water often lessens the sense of fright.

Baby Clothing

• Inexpensive, long-lasting baby bibs can be made from flannel-backed oil cloth. For those lovely bibs people love to give as gifts, protect with a good coating of spray starch. Your baby can dribble and gurgle food all he wants, and the stains will still wash out.

• When you accidently break the adhesive tab on a disposable diaper, use masking tape instead to hold the diaper.

• Dull diaper pins will go through cloth more easily if dipped into a bar of soap first.

• A little cooking oil added to the rinse water will keep rubber baby clothes soft and pliable.

• A dry cleaning bag makes life with baby easier when travelling. Keep one in your diaper bag. When changing the baby away from

136

home you have a handy protective cloth. But keep it out of baby's reach.

• Rolled-up receiving blankets make great bolsters for your baby's stroller. They will keep him from sliding from side-to-side.

• Attach a towel rack to the end of your baby's crib or bed. Use it to hang those frequently needed items. It saves you steps and as a bonus, makes moving the crib or bed easier. The towel rack serves as a handle.

• You can mend torn crib sheets without sewing. Use iron-on patches and decals.

• To keep the feet in children's pajamas free of dust and grime, have the children wear old socks over them.

• Tired of losing small baby clothes in the washing machine? Make a washing bag out of nylon net. Stuff in all those little socks and what have you. Close the bag with a safety pin.

• When storing children's clothes from one season to another, unstitch the hems and the cuffs. When another season rolls around all you have to do is have your children try on the clothes as you pin for the appropriate length.

• When your children are close in age and you have trouble sorting out their clothes—especially underwear and socks—number the clothes with indelible ink. One for the oldest child, two for the second and so on.

• Dressing time goes faster and easier if you hang your children's clothes in sets. The underwear, socks, pants, shirts needed for each day of the week all together.

• A covered cigar box is excellent for keeping a little girl's hair ribbons, barrettes and pins in one place. No more hunting around in drawers at the last minute.

• To help children learn good grooming habits, hang a full-length mirror in a handy place. The average mirror is adult height, and children will never learn if they can't see.

• Ordinary ball point pens can be used to cover small white spots that appear in jeans.

Shoes

• The eyelets in baby shoes will not mark the laces if you coat them with clear nail polish.

• Here's a way to prevent the tongues of children's shoes from slipping down: Cut two parallel notches in each tongue. Before tying, slip the laces through the notches.

• When polishing children's open-work sandals, wear thin nylon gloves. The polish will stay on the shoes and not on your hands.

• To avoid stroller scuff marks on children's shoes, secure a piece of carpeting to the foot rest portion.

• Give your child's freshly shined shoes a good coating of hair spray. Not only will the shine last longer, but scuffs and scratches are also less likely to appear.

• When your children are learning to put their shoes on by themselves, mark the sole of one shoe in some distinctive manner. A line of red nail polish on the left, for example. This way, your child will know just by looking which is which.

• Wipe children's white shoes that are grass stained with a ball of cotton that has been saturated with peroxide.

• As your children learn to polish their own shoes, give them an old powder puff to bring out the shine. The tape makes it easier for children to hold.

• You don't really need liquid white polish for baby shoes. Wipe them off with rubbing alcohol and then polish with clear shoe wax. Buff as you would ordinarily.

Baby Food and Feeding

• You can make your own baby food by using the puree speed on your blender. Toss in adult foods, turn the blender on and let it go. To keep homemade baby food fresh, freeze it in ice cube trays.

• Commercial baby food can be heated over the pilot light of your gas stove.

• Six-pack cardboard carrying cartons make great baby bottle holders for your refrigerator. Keeps the bottles in one place.

• Your baby will have a better grip on his bottle, especially a glass one, if you wrap it with masking tape.

• Tired of squinting at the ounce lines on bottles? Mark them with nail polish at two ounce intervals.

• A few rubber bands wrapped around baby's bottle or glass or cup will provide a good grip and prevent spills.

• A metal coffee can makes a good bottle warmer and prevents pot damage.

• To keep your saucepans from corroding when heating or sterilizing bottles, add a few agate marbles. This also works in sterilizers.

• You can remove hard water sediment from baby bottles by soaking them in white vinegar. To save brushing bottles out, try shaking. Put white bread crumbs into the bottles and add water. Shake hard and rinse in warm water.

- When you have trouble removing the lid on a jar of baby food, puncture a small hole in the lid. This releases the air so the lid twists off with ease.
- Cooling down too warm bottles is a snap if you keep some extra formula on ice in the refrigerator. Whenever you find yourself with a bottle too hot to handle, pour in some of the chilled formula. In a splash, the liquid is the right temperature.

Kids' Food

- Kids just naturally love hotdogs, but add the bun and it's too large for their mouths. Forget the standard hotdog roll. Use a refrigerated biscuit. You can roll it out as thin as you like. When it's baked, add the hotdog.
- Instead of just frying eggs for your children, change the shape. Put some open end cookie cutters in the frying pan. Then add the eggs. The white will spread into the shape of the cutter and your child will be fascinated with the different shapes.
- Kids prefer to sweeten their own food, but they often get carried away with the amount. They also tend to spill sugar all over the table. Keep sugar in a salt shaker. Makes the whole process easier.
- For a different school lunch, put hot soup in a thermos and add an uncooked hotdog or two. By lunchtime the franks are cooked and deliciously warm.
- Fussy eaters can often be enticed to eat their food if you add a few drops of vegetable coloring. Pink mashed potatoes are particularly popular.
- Decorate hot cereal with bits and pieces of chopped fruits like raisins, dates, apricots. This trick is especially good for children who are not too anxious to eat the fruit they need.

Boosters

- When you use the old standby, telephone books, to boost your child up to table height, be sure to cover them with plastic wrap. Any accidental spills or drops won't get the telephone books dirty.
- A fast and inexpensive booster seat is a plastic wastepaper basket. Cut away about one-third of the side and add a pillow of appropriate height. And best of all, this booster seat is so light, you can take it visiting with you.
- You can encourage children to finish their milk by adding a maraschino cherry. To reach the sweet tidbit, they have to drink the milk—or at least most of it!
- There's no need to toss out a leftover tablespoon or two of baby

food. Accumulate these leftovers into one jar. Every few days treat your baby to a meal of leftovers.

• TV trays make great dishes for children. If a tray falls to the floor during mealtime, it's not your good dish that goes crashing.

Health and Safety

• While sanding brand new baby shoes helps to prevent slips and slides, nothing really works like a thin layer of foam rubber. Just glue a piece to the sole of the shoe. As it wears thin, remove it with a single edged razor blade and glue on a new sheet.

• When even adults have been known to walk through solid glass doors, imagine what children are likely to do. Mark your glass doors with decals or colored tape at child eye level.

• Is your child at the creeping crawling stage? Help keep your lamps where they belong—on the table. Secure the lamps and cords to the table legs with string.

• To keep lids of all kinds from smashing small curious fingers, secure half inch pieces of cork to the lids. Even if a lid does fall, it will stop short of smashed fingers.

• If your toddler is inclined to sneak outside when you're not looking, hang a bell on your door. Whenever the door is opened, you will be notified.

• Some children, when first promoted from crib to bed, tend to roll over in their sleep and fall out of the bed. To prevent injury, leave the old crib mattress on the floor beside the bed at night. Should your child roll out, the crib mattress will break the fall.

• To keep children from locking themselves in the bathroom, keep a small hand towel across the top of the door. Urge all adults to replace the towel when they leave the bathroom.

• A rubber pad attached to the seat of a high chair will keep your baby from sliding out.

• You can keep a high chair from tipping over with an ordinary screen door hook and eye. Insert the eye part into a wall and attach the hook to the back of the baby's high chair. When in use, just make the hook-up.

• Another tip-over prevention hint: Attach corks to the front rungs of your child's rocking chair.

• To make sure small fingers never get mashed in the car door, ask your children to put their hands on their heads until you have closed and locked the doors. Kids are especially responsive to this safety measure when it becomes a game along the lines of "Show how you put your hands on your head..."

• If you are out of covers for unused electrical sockets, cellophane or masking tape will work quite well as a temporary measure.

• You can mask the taste of most liquid medicines by mixing them with grape juice. Capsules and pills are taken with less fuss when mixed with warm cereal, pudding or apple sauce. When measuring out liquid medicine, give it to your child in a larger spoon. If you need a teaspoon, measure the teaspoon and then transfer it to a tablespoon. Two benefits to this trick—your child feels he is getting less of the awful stuff, and the bigger spoon makes spills less likely.

• When you have to check inside your child's mouth, use a lollipop as a tongue depressor.

Warning Signs

• Identify the hot water faucets in your home by painting them red. This is a color children quickly learn to recognize. And while on the subject of red, you can't keep your poisonous household cleaners and detergents locked away forever. Mark dangerous ones like bleach, ammonia, and what have you, with big red circles. Nail polish or paint does well. Explain to your child the need to recognize this mark as a warning.

• And for the various chemicals used in today's home, keep an antidote list in a convenient place. Also the telephone numbers of the police, fire department and poison control center if there is one in your area.

Sick in Bed

• When your child is confined to bed, feeding can be a problem. You can make a sturdy temporary bed tray from a cardboard box. Cut away enough board from the long side so that the box fits over the child's legs.

• When bringing your child a tray of food, use a damp paper towel as a place mat. The damp towel will serve as a grip for the tray or dishes.

• Find yourself with an assortment of medicine bottles to help your child over an illness? You can keep all together if you use a muffin tin. It also makes a convenient carrying tray as you go into the sick room to dispense medication.

Safety First!!

• Is a particular toy small enough for your child to swallow? Here's a reliable rule of thumb: If the toy is bigger than your child's fist, then the toy is too big to be swallowed.

• A distraught, frightened child can usually be calmed if you whisper. The soothing sounds relax even the most uptight child.

Toys, Games, and Playing
• Crayons can be sharpened quickly if you dip the end into hot water and then reform the point by rolling the crayon between your thumb and forefinger.

• Empty band aid tins are great for storing crayons.

• A mirror placed near your child's crib or playpen keeps him interested for quite a while.

• Pipe cleaners, especially the colored ones, are inexpensive amusing playthings for children from age four up.

• An empty thread spool tied to the end of a balloon makes it easier for the child to hold.

• Remember, most children are unimpressed by expensive, complicated toys. Simple is usually better. Empty spools of thread can be strung into necklaces. Children can also paint these spools, and string them as Christmas tree decorations. Empty plastic cottage and sour cream containers are fine sand toys. Empty milk and cream cartons with the tops removed are terrific building blocks. Empty tissue boxes can be strung together for a pull-toy.

• An old truck tire—available at most junk yards—can be filled with sand to make a sand box. The rim serves as a comfy seat.

• A shoe bag attached to a child's playpen or bed becomes a handy storage area for small toys and such.

• When your child reaches the throwing stage, you can save yourself many a bend over if you attach strings to the various toys and secure the strings to the playpen or high chair or crib. When the toy gets tossed out, your child will soon learn how to get it back all alone.

• A large powder puff is a good blackboard eraser. And for a quick blackboard, paint a piece of wallboard black.

Toy Care
• Stuffed toys can be dry cleaned. Rub dry cornstarch into the toy. Let it stand for an hour and then brush the starch off.

• If you add a drop or two of glycerin to soap-bubble solution, the bubbles come out colored.

• When plastic toys are out of shape, soak them in hot water. When the plastic is soft enough, work them back into shape.

• The best bath for toys is baking soda solution. After washing, the toys can go right back into small mouths without any danger of the child ingesting something harmful.

- Cardboard games will last longer if you coat them with shellac.
- Empty baking soda cans make good pencil holders for children. They can be covered with foil or construction paper.
- Empty coffee cans, the ones with plastic lids, make nice toy drums. They are also quieter than commercial drums.
- Tin pie plates can be made into tambourines. Punch holes in the rim. String buttons and tie through the holes.

Glue Ideas

- If you soak plain tapioca in water you will get a harmless, odorless, and stainless glue for children to use. You can let your children use it without worrying about what will happen if they taste it.
- To keep paint and glue pots from tipping over, cut a hole in the center of a sponge. Insert the pot into the hole. If your child has a regular play table, glue the sponge to the surface.
- Modeling clay is easier to work with if a child's hands are given a thin coating of petroleum jelly first. Store modeling clay in aluminum foil to keep it from drying out.
- Wrapping new crayons in masking tape will keep them from breaking.
- To keep paste smooth and fresh, moisten the lid with a little water before screwing the top back to the jar.
- If you paste rubber rings along your child's toy shelf, the rubber balls will stay in place without falling to the floor.

Make Your Own

- When you find yourself having to blow up a lot of toys, attach your vacuum cleaner hose to the exhaust end. The exhaust air will do the huffing and puffing for you.
- Plastic egg cartons make fine display trays for the assortment of dead bugs and beetles most children insist collecting at one point or another in their lives. The lid can be closed firmly so you don't have to view the specimen collection.
- You can make your own jigsaw puzzles. Select a picture from a magazine, paste it onto a piece of cardboard, and cut it into a variety of shapes and sizes.
- The plastic lids from cans of baking soda and coffee can be used as wheels when your children are making things. The wheels can be secured with brass fasteners available in any stationery store. These lids can also be painted red and black and used for a giant checker

set.

• Your child need not miss a favorite bedtime story just because you'll be away for the evening. Record a story on tape. At bedtime, the sitter can flip on your tape recorder. Not only will your child be happy, but your sitter will be, too.

• An old mattress covered with denim makes a fine bouncing place for children—it may just keep them off the furniture.

• What to do with all the children's artwork? It certainly builds up. Drawings and paintings can be protected with a good coating of hair spray. This will keep them from fading and the colors will not wear off. For easier display, hang a fishnet on one wall. Any drawings and paintings can then be suspended from the net by clothespins or hooks. And your walls will not be damaged with nails or pieces of tape.

• A not so sliding slide can be waxed up again quite easily. Just rub sheets of waxed paper, vigorously, up and down the shoot. This method will not leave stains on clothing.

• Take a sheet from a calendar and paste it on a piece of cardboard. Then put the dates into neat little squares. This collection of number squares is a big help when teaching your children the basics of arithmetic. And, of course, you can use several calendar sheets.

"Kissing It Better" Ideas

• When you have to remove a splinter, apply an ice cube to the skin first. The cold temporarily numbs the area and the splinter can be extracted with less pain.

• Before applying a band aid to a cut or scratch, gently shave away the hair on the surrounding skin. Part of the pain of removing band aids is the fact that the adhesive sticks to the skin hair. When removing the band aid, apply a generous amount of oil—any kind will do whether baby or cooking oil. This will dissolve the adhesive.

• Babies who have difficulty falling asleep generally miss their mothers. But they don't necessarily have to feel her arms around them. Quite often they are comforted if they can "smell her". Make a point of wearing a favorite cologne during the day. Spray this scent freely around your baby's crib. Then when you pop the little one into the crib, that old familiar scent will be right there as an added measure of security.

• A common worry for mothers of very young babies is whether or not the baby's head will get stuck between crib slats. Crib liners are all too easy to push to one side. To eliminate this worry, buy fabric about thirty-six inches wide and weave it through the slats and secure to the front and back of the crib with thumbtacks. By the time the baby is strong enough to push the fabric down, his head will be too big to go through the slats.

• Babies love to show their appreciation of a good meal by spitting up. To keep a wee one sweet smelling, this means a constant change of shirts and tops. But not if you wipe the mess away with a cloth dipped in a solution of baking soda water. Not only does the odor disappear but the stain does, too.

• Ever notice how babies seem to howl when they are put back in their cribs after a feeding? Well, why not? How would you feel about getting back into a cold bed? To keep the crib warm, cozy, and inviting, lay a heating pad or hot water bottle on the mattress whenever you take the baby out for a feeding or a change.

• Children will be less frightened and, therefore, more co-operative during their first hair cut if they know what's going on first. An electric razor approximates the sound of the barber's equipment. Several weeks before the first tonsorial visit, introduce your child to this sound. Run the razor over your own skin so that the child sees that it does not hurt.

• Washing hair for small children can be a panic in more ways than one. Essentially the problem is that they don't want to get their faces wet. Try the kitchen sink for the next shampoo. Have the child lie on the kitchen drainboard and use the spray attachment for wetting and rinsing. Some children prefer to lie on their backs, others on their stomachs.

• To trim bangs quickly and accurately, wet the hair thoroughly. Push any hair you don't want to cut behind the ears and secure with pins. Place a piece of cellophane tape across the bangs. The top edge of the tape should be your cutting line. Snip away. Presto! A neat, straight trim, and best of all, no hair to sweep up. You just remove the cellophane tape and drop it in the wastepaper basket.

Travelling

• A few days before a long automobile trip, keep your children on a light-foods diet. Heavy foods increase the likelihood of car sickness. Bring along a supply of fresh oranges. They tend to settle rolling stomachs.

• A plastic laundry basket stuffed with a pillow makes a fine travelling crib for an infant.

CHAPTER 21

PETS IN PARTICULAR AND ANIMALS IN GENERAL

Birds

• When using ammonia or other strong-smelling products, remove your bird to another room. The fumes can harm your feathered friends. And when repainting the birdcage, use a non-toxic paint.

Canary Care

• Your canary not up to tune? Try a small piece of rock candy in its water dish. The sugar gets them back in voice.

• Always spilling the seed when putting food in your bird's dish? Transfer the seed from the original box to an empty salt box. That little spout makes the pouring much easier.

• Shirt cardboards make a good subsitute for lining paper. They last longer, too.

• Don't discard the outside leaves of a head of lettuce. Let your bird have the benefit.

• If your bird isn't too crazy about taking a bath, sprinkle a few seeds over the bath water. That should tempt him in. And put a little gravel at the bottom. Bird experts claim that the slippery bottom is what discourages aviary hygiene.

• Spilled bird seed can be picked up with a damp paper towel.

• Have a broken umbrella? Don't throw it out. Remove the spokes and use it as a birdcage cover at night.

Wild Bird Friends

• Love your outside birdbath, but hate the slime that builds up? Empty the bath and scrub the slime away, using water and a small amount of household bleach. Rinse well with clear water. Let the empty bath stand in the sun for several hours so all the chlorine will evaporate. Now line the bath with clear plastic wrap and fill. No more bottom slime. The wrap can be discarded each time you add fresh water.

• The birds not stopping at your bath? Is it the sun? Move it to the shade. Water exposed to direct sunlight is too warm.

• Another thing that attracts birds to your bath are a few shiny, colorful marbles at the bottom. Or those colored stones used in fish tanks. The flashing color catches the attention of your flying friends.

• Want a wintertime treat for the birds? Try leaving blobs of peanut butter sprinkled with seed around your yard. It's a nice change from the usual suet. So are dried orange halves.

• Bird marks on the canvas covers used for your outdoor furniture? Use a stiff-bristled brush to apply a mixture of yellow soap and dry washing soda. Rinse with your hose and sun dry.

• Like birds but not in your garden? Put a few navy or split peas in a balloon and blow it up. Tie the balloon to a short stick in your garden. The slightest breeze will cause the beans to rattle and chase the birds away.

• Bags of moth flakes tied to the rafters of your garage and from the gutters of your house will discourage birds.

Cats

• Want to give your cat a cleaning without water? Rub him thoroughly with uncooked cornmeal. Brush or comb the meal. Presto! A sweet-smelling cat all shiny and clean.

• If you stuff a moth ball or two behind the cushions of your furniture, your cat will stay on the ground.

• Cats need to sharpen their claws, but not on your furniture or drapes. Nail a piece of firewood to a stand. It makes a great scratching post.

Dogs

• Dogs can be "dry cleaned" with baking soda. Rub the soda in thoroughly and brush or comb out. Removes doggy smells, too.

• If you bathe your dog in a shower or tub, put a wad of steel wool in the drain to catch the hairs. No more clogged pipes.

• For an extra soft and shiny after-bath coat, add two tablespoons of baking soda to both wash and rinse water. Cream rinse for your hair is great for poodles. A little lemon juice or vinegar added to the rinse water will neutralize doggy odors.

• When bathing your dog, put cotton in its ears and a drop of castor oil in each eye. These precautions will keep water out of its ears and soap out of its eyes. And a rubber bathmat at the bottom of the tub will keep it from slipping around.

• Your dog will shed less if you lubricate his coat with olive oil, coconut oil or lanolin every ten days to two weeks.

Cat and Dog Care

• You can remove pet hairs from your furniture quickly and completely if you use a damp chamois cloth.

• If your pet has fleas, take him outside and sprinkle him thoroughly with salt. Brush or comb away the salt. (Not recommended if pet has sensitive or broken skin.) If you sprinkle salt around the dog house or cat basket, it will keep fleas away. So will pine needles—fresh ones, of course. Old foam-rubber auto seat cushions, cut to size, make excellent beds for your pets. Ticks and fleas cannot settle in them.

• To remove burrs from your cat's or dog's hair, work oil into the tangle with your fingers. . .or you can crush the burr with a pair of pliers. Once crushed, the burr loses its holding power and can be combed out.

• To remove ticks, soak a cotton swab with cleaning fluid and dab on the head of the tick. Pull it out carefully with tweezers. You can also soak each tick with alcohol. Remove with tweezers gently.

• Skunk odors can be washed away with tomato juice or a vinegar and water solution.

• To keep pet dishes from skidding all over the place, glue a strip of rubber around the bottom.

• Dry food is tastier for your dog if you add a boullion cube that has been dissolved in a bit of boiling water.

• Crying puppies and kittens can be calmed if you place a ticking clock wrapped in a small towel nearby. A young animal newly separated from its mother can also be calmed with a hot water bottle wrapped in a towel.

• Chewing can be discouraged if you apply a little oil of cloves (which can be found in most drug stores) to the furniture. A thoroughly rinsed out plastic bottle also makes a nice chew toy.

A General Safety Tip For Cats and Dogs

• Wrap a piece of reflector tape on his collar so drivers can see him more easily at night.

General Cat and Dog Accident Tips

• Blot up as much of the moisture as you possibly can. Rub the spot with a solution of vinegar or lemon juice mixed with warm, sudsy water. Keep blotting the spot. Next, pour club soda, straight from the bottle, over the spot. Place towels over the spot until almost dry.

Fish

• Do they keep leaping out of the tank? Take a piece of nylon netting and place it over the tank. Secure with a rubber band.

148

CHAPTER 22

SICKROOM TIPS

Basic Precautions: Keep a list of all emergency telephone numbers by the telephone. Type the numbers...police, fire department, doctor, poison control center, etc...on a 3x5 card and coat with clear nail polish. This not only gives the card extra strength but it also keeps it clean. Punch a small hole in the upper left hand corner. Run a wire bread wrapper through the hole and secure the card to the cord of your telephone. Should you ever need the card, it will be readily available.

• Start your own medical file for your entire family. A looseleaf notebook, index tabbed, for each family member is ideal. With a handy notebook kept up-to-date, you will not be forced to rely on memory. When filling out medical and/or insurance forms, you will be surprised at how much time you save by just flipping open a notebook and copying off the information...which is almost certain to be correct.

• Keep a quarter taped to the inside of your automobile glove compartment. You will always have the change to summon emergency aid should you need it while on the road.

• Teaching children to prepare for emergencies is never easy, but you can try. Along with a clean handkerchief, an indentification card should go into a pocket every morning. Write your child's name, address, telephone number, blood type, allergies, and doctor's name and number on a card and slip it into a plastic holder used for luggage tags. The card stays clean and the plastic is less likely to slip from a child's pocket.

Medication: Whether dosing yourself or someone else with medicine, it is a serious responsibility. Always read the labels carefully and follow the directions. And, too, make a point of asking your pharmacist if there are foods that should not be taken while on any medication. Some medicines, for example, are neutralized when taken with dairy products.

• When medicine must be taken at stated intervals, an ordinary kitchen timer can often serve as a handy portable "alarm clock". The family "nurse" can carry it with her and forget about watching the clock. And since the timer is close by, there is no chance that she will not hear it when it goes off.

• When pouring out bottled medicines, keep the label facing up. This way, any drips or spills will not ooze over the label and make the directions hard to read.

• Pill swallowing can be a chore at times, especially for small children. If your doctor allows, pills and tablets can be mashed and mixed with small amounts of pudding or gelatin for easier swallowing.

• Although most liquid medicines are flavored to disguise any unpleasant taste, some people still taste the stuff. Before taking the medicine, rinse your mouth with ice water. The cold water will temporarily numb the taste buds on your tongue. And, since half of tasting is smelling, hold your nose as you take a swig.

Temperature Taking: When you must use a rectal thermometer, moisten a ball of cotton with baby oil and then wipe the thermometer with it. The whole process will be that much less uncomfortable.

• Alcohol is an excellent disinfectant for all types of thermometers. When a patient's temperature must be taken several times a day, leave a glass filled with alcohol in a handy place. After each temp-taking, just place the thermometer in the alcohol. This saves having to sterilize the instrument after each use.

• Mercury in home thermometers has been known to divide. If this happens to you, don't toss the thermometer out. Just run a magnet along the bulb end. This will draw the mercury together.

Home Nursing Ideas: An ordinary muffin tin makes a great medicine tray. Arrange all the bottles and containers, one to each muffin tray, and carry it with you as needed.

• To prevent bedside table crowding while sick in bed, hang a shoe bag with at least six pockets by the bed. This makes a dandy holder for tissues, eye glasses, combs, all the little things that might just be needed.

Keeping the Patient Comfortable: Plastic bags from the dry cleaners can be used for emergency rubber sheets.

• Need a non-spill drinking glass for the patient? Take any empty eight ounce jar and make a hole in the lid. Fill the jar with the necessary liquid, screw the lid on, and insert a drinking straw...a flexible one if it is available. The hole should be slightly larger than the straw to allow air in while drinking.

• A light-weight serving tray for meals in bed can be made quickly and easily with two aluminum roasting pans. Place the pans bottom-to-bottom and secure together. This can be done by poking holes in the aluminum and then securing the pans with string, fine wire, or even those metal paper clasps that spread apart. Once the pans are together, cut away enough metal from the long sides of one pan—enough so that it will slip easily over the patient's legs. Food dishes are then placed in the portion which has not been cut away.

• When you have someone who must have a bedpan, rinse it in hot water first—to take the chill off it.

• Sick people tend to get sick to their stomachs and that can mean a messy clean-up. Not if you have a supply of empty coffee cans with the plastic lids close at the bedside. The coffee can serves its purpose, the lid is snapped on—and instant, odorless disposal.

• When your patient wants an alcohol rub-down, put the liquid in a sprinkle top bottle and sprinkle away. The odor of the alcohol can be masked by adding a few drops of your favorite cologne or toilet water. And you can also take the chill off the alcohol if you run the container under warm water for a few minutes.

• Bedsores on your patient? Ease the discomfort this way: Take a soft, rubber powder puff and cut a hole in the center, larger than the sore. Slip the puff under the affected area.

• If you apply baby oil to adhesive tape, it comes off with less pain. And nail polish remover takes off marks left by adhesive tape. After using the polish remover, wash the spot and apply a liberal dose of your favorite hand cream or lotion.

• Applying compresses, whether hot or cold, can be a messy, time consuming task. Try this method: When the compress must be warm, cover it with a filled hot water bottle and secure with a towel. So long as the hot water bottle is warm, the compress will stay that way. For cold compresses, use an ice bag, again, secured with a towel.

Keeping the Germs Under Control: One family member sick is bad enough. The last thing you need is to have the illness spread. You will lessen the chances if you...

• Have the patient use paper plates and plastic eating utensils for the duration. They can be tossed into the trash.

• Line a wastepaper basket with a plastic bag. All used tissues and other used paper products go into the bag. When filled, tie the bag off and into the trash...germs and all.

CHAPTER 23

HOBBIES, SPORTS AND PASTIMES

We all have our ways to relax, but sometimes the relaxant causes more frustration than it relieves. Look these hints over. They may serve to make your pleasure pleasurable.

Art...*Painting:* A weekend dabbler with the paints and brushes? Have you tried any of these ideas?

• When the paint in a tube dries causing the cap to stick, hold the tube over a lighted match for a few seconds.

• Aluminum trays for frozen foods make great containers for mixing paints. So do plastic egg containers.

• After you are done with your artistic efforts and have cleaned your brushes, coat them with a minute amount of petroleum jelly. This will keep the bristles soft.

Books: Whether your library is for enjoyment or investment or both, the following will help to keep your books readable for years to come:

• Imitation leather and plastic book covers will not crack if they are given a thin coating of petroleum jelly from time-to-time.

• Book covers can also be coated with shellac. Any dust accumulation wipes right off.

• If you have to "wash" your book covers, use a clean, soft cloth that has been dipped in a solution of two parts water and one part white vinegar. Wring the cloth out and wipe quickly.

• Rubbing your book covers with waxed paper helps keep them clean.

• Spotted pages? Wrap a piece of extra fine sandpaper around a sanding block. Go over the spots slowly and gently with the paper until they disappear.

• You won't have fungus or mildew problems if you keep a piece of charcoal on each bookcase shelf...or you can keep an electric light burning on each shelf. (This last hint is suitable only for very rare and valuable books...unless, of course, you own the power company.)

• Should you find fungus or mildew on your books, wipe the affected area with a clean, soft cloth that has been moistened with rubbing alcohol.

Fishing: Before you can do any fishing, you need bait...

• Soak walnut shells that have been crushed in three gallons of water for several hours. Splash the water over dirt. Within fifteen minutes many, many worms will work their way to the surface.

• Coffee grounds sprinkled on the dirt brings angleworms up.

• Add a teaspoon of dry mustard to a cup and a half of water. Pour the water on the dirt—the worms will be attracted to the surface.

• Puncture a beer or soda can in several places and leave it in shallow water. Within an hour or so, a lot of small, soft-shelled crayfish will have moved inside.

• Packing live minnows in wet grass keeps them alive until you need them...or at least for a few hours.

• And when you have trouble securing bait, miniature marshmallows do the trick as well as worms.

Fish Hooks: Tired of hooks in your fingers? Dip the tip of each in water-soluble glue.

• Keep your hooks in a piece of cork...keeps them out of your fingers. When not using the hooks, stick them in a cork and store them in a jar of baking soda.

Fishing Rods: To protect the wood, rinse the rod after each use and coat with paste wax.

• Used flashlight batteries can be effective as bobbers.

Cleaning Fish: Here are a few ideas on how to make a messy job less so.

• For fish that have been out of the water for a while, the easiest way to scale them is to dip them in boiling water.

• A stiff wire brush or a dull knife also works well as these methods do not damage the meat.

• Use an ordinary clip board when cleaning fish. Clip the fish to the board by the tail and it will stay secure.

• And finally, tired of dropping keys and other goodies overboard and having them disappear into the briny deep?- Anything that you don't want to lose, secure to a cork. If you drop it overboard, it will float.

Golf: Rub your wooden golf club handles with shoe polish occasionally and they will keep their luster.

• Rust, dirt, and grime can be cleaned from golf clubs with aluminum foil...or you can use a damp sponge and baking soda.

Hunting: Waterfowl are easier to pluck if dipped in a bucket of boiling water to which two tablespoons of detergent have been added. Rinse the bird and pluck away.

• For those who wear hunting boots, pull a pair of cotton socks over your wool ones. The cotton pair will absorb the moisture that condenses on the rubber and keep your wool socks dry.

Ice Skating: You can keep the blades of your skates rust-free during the off-season if you rub them with a bit of petroleum jelly and store them in plastic bags.

Photography: Basic to every shutterbug is a camera so...
- Since cold weather congeals oil which can slow camera-shutter speeds, keep your camera under your coat in the winter.
- The glare on a shiny object can be reduced with a coat of hair spray before you start shooting.
- When you clean your lenses, don't forget to clean the cap. A dirty lens cap only grimes the lens itself.
- For that extra ounce of protection, wrap your camera in an old nylon stocking before putting it back in its case.

Photographs: And how to protect the finished product...
- When you put pictures in an album, slip the negative behind the print. You'll always know where to find it.
- Dirty photographs? They can be wiped clean with soft white bread...or dampen a soft cloth with warm water and sprinkle on a few drops of ammonia. Wring the cloth almost dry and quickly wipe the photographs. Dry immediately with a soft, clean cloth.
- When showing slides do you sometimes feel silly because one is upside down? No need anymore. Mark each slide in the upper left hand corner with a dab of red nail polish. So long as the red drops are to the upper left, the slide is in correctly.

Records: Wondering how to sort your records? How about by subject? And then run a stripe of colored tape along the back edge of each album. Maybe blue for blues music, green for vocals, etc. No more rooting around, you just pull out the albums color-taped for what you want.

Stamps: Used stamps can be removed from envelopes with a drop or two of lighter fluid. Apply the fluid to the back of the stamp from the inside of the envelope.

Swimming: If you rub a small amount of mineral or olive oil over your eye lids and lashes before swimming the salt or chlorinated water will be less irritating.

Tennis: Real cat-gut tennis rackets can be preserved for longer life if the string is coated with petroleum jelly.

CHAPTER 24

ODDS AND ENDS

And finally, an assortment of real odd ones for the end. Those weird problems that seem to defy solution and send our blood pressure up when we encounter them. Maybe your oddball problem is solved here...

Re-Use-Its:

• Those plastic containers that foods such as ricotta cheese come in, when empty, are nice storage containers for things like children's modeling clay, loose crayons and such.

• The plastic caps on squeeze bottles of dish detergent come in very handy as funnels for filling salt and pepper shakers.

• Don't throw out shoebox lids. They can be used to reinforce the bottom of a paper or plastic shopping bag. And if you place a shoebox lid in the bottom of your canvas tote, the tote will stay open so you can drop things in quickly.

• Every cleaning closet holds an assortment of plastic bottles with pump tops. When the bottles are empty, rinse them out and fill them with liquid furniture polish, ammonia, things like that. Now have your other cleaning products ready for a quick touch-up squirt. Just be sure to relabel the bottles.

Leak Prevention:

• Tired of wax containers that drip all over your refrigerator? It need never happen again. Wrap the bottom of each container with a piece of aluminum foil.

• Not exactly a leak, but when you drop an egg it makes a mess. If you moisten your fingertips before reaching for an egg, you won't drop it...instant mess prevention.

Emergency Tips:

• Your car windshield covered with snow and you don't have a scraper? Use a plastic credit card. The sharp edge really cuts through the ice, sleet, and snow.

• When your lights go out and you need a flashlight to see what's what, point it toward the ceiling for maximum illumination. The light reflects off the white paint.

• And who likes wasting time poking for a flashlight in a dark drawer? Paint the bottom portion with luminous paint and you will be able to spot it immediately.

Keep Its:

• If you wrap a rubber band around the lower portion of your cigarette lighter it won't slip out of your pocket.

• To preserve the original color of anything made of real linen, wrap it in BLUE tissue paper. This also works for those important documents we all need. Blue tissue paper prevents them from turning yellow and going crumbly.

Loosen and Sharpen:

• Faced with a too-tight jar lid? Grasp the lid with a piece of sandpaper—it will open easily.

• When you first open a jar or bottle with sticky contents such as honey, molasses, nail polish, coat the threads of the bottle with a small amount of cooking oil. It won't stick shut after the oiling.

• You can sharpen a pair of scissors by cutting through a piece of sandpaper several times.

• Is your hand-operated can opener a bit on the dull side. Drop it in boiling water for several minutes.

Memo Minders:

• Always writing yourself notes and forgetting where you put the reminders? You won't again if you attach the memo to your pack of cigarettes or cigars or pipe tobacco.

• How often do you forget to send out greeting cards? Here's a way to always remember: At the beginning of each year, buy all the cards you will need. Sign, address, and stamp them. Then clip the January ones to that calendar page, the February ones, and so forth. On the first of each month, drop all the cards in the mail. So a birthday card may arrive a week or two early! That only proves the person is really on your mind.

Decorating Thoughts:

• When you have candles about only for decoration, coat them with clear shellac. They won't melt during a heat wave, and they will be easier to clean.

• Always hang your mirrors away from direct sunlight. If you don't, the glass becomes cloudy looking after a while.

Check It Out:

• Do you suspect your bathroom scale of being off by several pounds? Place a five-pound bag of flour or sugar on the scale and see what the results are.

• That checkbook just won't balance? Divide the difference between what you show and the bank shows by nine. If nine goes in evenly, there is a very good chance you have transposed a figure. Or maybe the bank did. Check it out.

Envelopes:

• Hate the taste of stamp glue? Lick the upper corner of the tasteless envelope instead.

• Make out your grocery list on an envelope and keep your cents-off coupons inside.

Key Easy:

• Getting locked out of a car or a house is a common problem. It also makes you feel a bit silly. You can avoid the problem from now on by carrying an extra set of keys in the zipper section of your handbag. You only need three keys, a house door key, car door key and trunk key. You'd be surprised how many people lock their car keys in the trunk.

• For harried husbands who dash out in the morning without their lunch, make a habit of dropping the car keys into the bag or box used to pack the lunch. If he doesn't remember the sandwich, he'll sure remember the keys.

• If you frame your door locks with reflector tape, just narrow strips, you won't waste time on chilly nights hunting blind for the keyhole.

• A lot of keys, a lot of worries, we are told. And one of those worries is trying to find the right key. Mark each key with a different colored paint. Red for the house, green for the cellar, etc. The tiny bottles of paint sold in hobby stores are perfect for this because there is such a wide variety of colors.

Ease-Its:

These hints are meant to remove some of life's more common frustrations:

• Slide a rubber bicycle handlebar grip over your mops and broom handles. Two advantages: You have a better grip when your hands are wet, and when you lean the mop or broom against a wall it won't fall to the floor.

• Tired of wanting to open your drapes by pulling at the close rope? Dot the pull that closes (or opens) your drapes with red nail polish. You'll always know which is which.

• Grocery shopping goes much faster if you make out your list in terms of the store's layout. If Aisle One is pet food, list that item first. You can do your shopping by going up one aisle and down another. No more dashing back and forth across the store.

• Here's another step-saver. Don't empty wastepaper baskets individually. Carry a large trash bag from room to room and empty the baskets into that.

• Alarm clock magic! The annoying ticking can be quieted if the clock rests on a dry sponge. Covering the clock with a glass bowl is another good idea. Do you sleep through an alarm clock? Rest the clock on an aluminum tray. When the alarm goes off, it will make an extra loud racket.

• Hot air heating registers have one annoying disadvantage. Things get dropped down them. And those things are hard to retrieve. Not if you remove the grate and line the opening with a piece of fine screening. There is no heat loss, but when something drops down the grate, the screen holds it.

• Insert a cup hook over your kitchen sink. When doing the dishes, hang your rings and wristwatch from the hook. No more hunting around later wondering just where you left your jewelry.

• Hang a curtain rod just outside your back door or in your porch. On rainy, wet days boots and shoes can be hung on the rod for drying. No more mud tracked through your clean house.

Save Its:

• Protect those favorite cigars from drying out. A few fresh apple peels added to the cigar box will keep the "smokes" from drying out.

• Has water spilled on your book? Place a blotter on each side of the wet page and press with an iron set for medium heat. Repeat until the page is smooth and dry. If several pages have been soaked, go over each one individually.

• And a final saver—for your back. No need to huff and puff to lift heavy pieces of furniture. Use an ordinary tire jack—the one you have in the trunk of your car!

INDEX

Alcoholic Beverages 30
Aluminum 67
Asparagus 4
Automobile Care 128-135
   Cleaning, 130
   Conserving Gasoline, 128
   Motor Maintenance, 134
   Safety, 128
   Summer Care, 129
   Tar Spots, 131
   Tires, 131
   Windows, 132
   Windshields, 132
   Winter Care, 129
Avocadoes 4

Bacon 4
Bananas 4
Bathroom 74
Beef 4
Beer 31
Belts .49
Biscuits 5, 25
Bleach 31
Blinds (see Shades)
Blood .31
Brass .67
Breads 25
Bronze 67
Brown Sugar 5
Butter 5, 31
Buttermilk 6
Buttons 56

Cabbage 6
Cakes 19-22
   Decorating, 21
   Serving, 20
Candle Wax 31
Canning 16-18
Carbon Paper 31
Casseroles 6
Catsup 6, 31
Cauliflower 6
Celery .7

Cheese .7
Chewing Gum 31
Chicken 7
Child Care 136-145
   Baby Clothing, 136
   Bath Time, 136
   Food & Feeding, 138
   Health & Safety, 140
   Shoes, 137
   Sick in Bed, 141
   Toy Care, 142
   Toy Making, 143
   Toys & Games, 142
   Travelling, 145
China .71
Chocolate 31
Chrome 67
Cigarette Burns 66
Cinnamon Toast 7
Cleaning Clues 73-74
Closets 43
Cod Liver Oil 31
Coffee 7, 32
Cookies 22-23
Cooking Oils 8
Copper 67
Corn 8
Cosmetics 32, 52
Cottage Cheese 8
Cream 8
Crystal 71
Curtain Care 83

Darning (see Sewing)
Doughnuts 8
Drawers 43
Drying Clothes 39

Eggs 8, 32
Energy Conservation 95-99
   Cooking, 96
   Electrical Appliances, 97
   Heating, 97
   Lights, 95
   Phone, 97
   Radiators, 98
   Refrigerators, 95

Wood Stoves, 198
Eyeglasses 50

Fingernails 51
Fireplaces 86
Fish....................9, 109
Floors 75-80
  Carpets, 77, 79
  Linoleum, 76
  Protection, 75
  Squeaky, 75
  Waxing, 76
  Woods, 75
Flowers & Plants 118-127
  Artificial, 122
  Cleaning, 119
  Cut Flowers, 121
  Cuttings, 119
  Garden Pests, 124
  Insecticides, 125
  Outdoor Gardening, 123
  Plant Problems, 120
  Transplanting, 126
  Watering & Nourshing, 118
  Weeds, 124
  Winter Flowers, 122
Freshness Hints 16
Furniture 62-66
  Cleaning, 62
  Polishing, 64

Garlic 9, 109
Gelatin 10
Gloves 45
Glue 32, 143
Grass 32
Grease 32
Gravy 10, 32

Hair Care 50
Ham 10
Handbags 46
Hats 45
Hobbies & Sports 152-154
  Art, 154
  Books, 152
  Fish, 153

Golf, 153
Hunting, 153
Ice Skating, 154
Photography, 154
Records, 154
Stamps, 154
Swimming, 154
Tennis, 154

Home Office Units 115-117
Hosiery..................46
Household Repairs 103-107
  Legs, 105
  Picture Hanging, 106
  Plaster, 105
  Plumbing, 104
  Rust, 103
  Screws, 104
  Tools, 103
  Walls, 105

Ice Cream.................33
Ink......................33
Ironing 41

Jams & Jellies 17, 33
Jewelry Care............53-55

Kitchen Hints 4-29
Knitting 60

Laundry 38-41
Leather..................62
Left-Overs 101
Lemons 10
Lettuce 11
Linoleum 76
Lipstick 33

Marble 68
Mending (see Sewing)
Mercurochrome...........33
Meringue 11
Metals 67-70
Milk.....................11
Mold & Mildew............33
Mud 34

160